joyce in the Belly of the Big Truck
A Modern Day Jonah Story

May this book be just one more tool for you on your journey. much Love, joyce

joyce a. cascio

Nineveh Press

Unity Church on the Lakeshore
41 S. Washington Street
P.O. Box 848
Douglas, MI 49406
269-857-8226

Copyright© 2004 by joyce a. cascio

All rights reserved.

Nineveh Press
Jefferson Street, Suite C-3 #272
Kearney, MO 64060

Cover by Charles Hackworth

Illustrations © 2000-2004 by Charles Hackworth

First Printing: October 2004

Printed in the United States of America

ISBN 0-9762373-0-X

The story you are about to read is true. However, some of the names have been changed to protect the privacy of those individuals or companies.

Acknowledgements

Thank you, Holley Reynolds for your editing, dedication, and commitment to this book. This book would not be what it is without you.

Thank you, Charles Hackworth for your artistic contributions. Your work has captured profoundly, the essence of each chapter.

Huge thanks to all of my family and friends who have supported me throughout this process, and whose presence in my life has helped to make this book possible.

Thank you, Matt Cascio and Seth Cascio for teaching me many valuable life lessons. I am forever grateful to you both.

Thank you, Amanda Cascio for all of your encouragement, devotion, and unwavering love. You have been an angel of light to my life all these years.

Thank you, God for your loving compassion and for giving me this story to live and to share with others. You remain my inspiration.

Contents

Foreword
9

Introduction
15

The Zen of Trucking
21

The Comparison Game
33

Invisible
43

Runaway Trains; Runaway Lives
53

Nowhere Land
65

Weapons of Mass Destruction
77

Objectified;
The Drive-Thru Window of Life
99

Letting Go
113

A Time to Forget; Independence Day
137

30 Pieces of Silver; Selling-Out
157

When No One is Watching
169

The Face of the Drifter;
The Cruelest Form of Abuse
177

Going Back to the Whale
193

The Nineveh Experience;
Opening My Heart to Love
205

About the Photographer
220

About the Author
221

Foreword

Story telling has been used for thousands of years as a way to inspire, share histories, give direction, or convey a way of life. It has also been used to instill taboos, social norms, and fear within an existing society. Most stories do not last beyond the first or second generations they were intended for. A few rare stories transcend their original audiences, taking on a life of their own, spanning hundreds, even thousands of years. The story of Jonah and the whale is such a story.

Only four chapters in length, the book of Jonah

is found in the Old Testament of the Bible, dating back sometime between the 5th and 8th centuries B.C. There is speculation whether Jonah actually existed, and whether his story is a metaphor or an actual event. One thing is certain: it is a story that has captivated the minds of children and adults for thousands of years.

The following is an account of how the story is *often* told:

A prophet, named Jonah, was asked by God to go and deliver a message to the people who lived in a city called Nineveh. However, Jonah was not interested in going to Nineveh. Instead, he decided to board a ship that sailed toward the city of Tarshish, and there he planned to hide from God. On the way to Tarshish, God caused a storm to prevent Jonah from reaching his destination. The ship's crew became terrified, believing they were all going to die at sea. However, Jonah remained asleep until he was awakened by the ship's captain. Jonah immediately identified the storm as a punishment from God for his disobedience. Jonah instructed the crew to throw him overboard in order to save themselves. They are reluctant to do this but as the storm continued to rage, all hope seemed to fade. Not wanting to perish in the storm, the crew tossed Jonah overboard, leaving him to the fate of his god. At this point a "big fish" appeared and swallowed Jonah. He remained in the belly of the "big fish" until he became remorseful, and asked God to pardon him for his disobedience—a total of 3 days.

Once Jonah asked for forgiveness and vowed to go to Nineveh, the whale "vomited" Jonah onto dry land. He proceeded to Nineveh and told the people that God was going to destroy. This caused the people of Nineveh to pray. Seeing this, God decided not to destroy them. Jonah was not pleased. He became angry with God. Jonah said to God something to the effect of, "Hey God, I told you before I came to Nineveh that there was no reason for me to come here, because I knew you would forgive these people. So, God, you go ahead and let me die right here! I am done! I have had it!"

Then Jonah walked to the eastside of the city gates and sat outside of them, waiting to see what God would decide. While Jonah sat pouting in the excruciating heat, God allowed a plant to grow up quickly and provide shade for Jonah's head, giving him comfort from the sun; Jonah was *grateful* for the plant. However, during the night, God allowed a worm to come and eat at the plant so that by morning it had died. The next day, the sun was so intense that Jonah nearly passed out from the heat. Again, Jonah, became angry with God, and decided he would rather die than live. God questioned Jonah about his ability to have pity for the life of a plant, but no pity for so many people and animals.

This is where the story ends: Jonah sitting quietly, having no response to God's question. The ending remains ambiguous as to what Jonah decides or to his fate.

Having so deeply identified with this man's story for most of my life, I decided to delve deeper into the "Jonah experience" to fully grasp its lessons. I did this by, asking myself, "What was Jonah's conflict?" Slowly the confusion and the inconsistencies of this story faded. Replaced with clarity, I stood staring into the face of Jonah's conflict, and I recognized Jonah's story was my own.

Today, for me, the story of Jonah is full of symbolism and compassion, having nothing to do with theology or ecclesiastical doctrines which had bound me so long to my fear and to the fears of others. As the story has transformed in my mind, a transformation began and continues within me. No longer a place of bondage, this story offers to me the liberation I have longed for my entire life.

Embracing new interpretations of the Jonah story, I finally had the key to unlock the door to the darkness I was harboring within myself. These insights did not come overnight, but were taught to me in a series of lessons that I now recognize as my own "Nineveh experience." That is when I realized the appeal and fascination of the Jonah story. Not only for me, but for millions, it was **real**. Jonah **did** exist, millions upon millions of times, because the Jonah story embodies the experience of every human being that has ever lived. "What is the Jonah experience?" you might ask. Each individual in their lifetime is asked by God to perform what seems to be an impossible task. "What is that task?" It is merely the same request that was asked of Jonah—that each of us must go to "Nineveh." Just as this request frightened Jonah, it terrifies us, because Nineveh is more than a city on a map, Nineveh represents the place of our greatest fear and dread. It is a place we could never fathom going on our own, and yet, that is exactly what God asks of us.

Like Jonah, each one of us chooses to run away, wanting to discover the city of Tarshish. The journey to Tarshish is long and hard, filled with betrayals, addictions, hardships, self-hatred, and all other forms of self-destruction. During this daring escape attempt, it never occurs to us that Tarshish, unlike Nineveh, *is not* a real place. It is merely a fantasy, a place we made-up in our minds to serve as a diversion, a distraction from our true course. It is real only in its representation of our intent and desire to escape from the presence of God at any cost, even our own demise.

However, God always intervenes in our moment of deepest despairing. This is why Jonah never reached Tarshish, and why we never will. Yes, the waters of our lives become troubled, not as punishment, but to help us return to the path of our original journey—*The Nineveh Experience.* To help guide us, God sends the whale. It may be in the form of a rehab center, a church, a new job, a relationship, maybe even prison. Whatever form the "whale" takes, at some point we recognize that we are not really alone. God has always been there in the mist of this experience with us.

We are relieved to know we are not going to drown. "But this?" we ask. "Inside the belly of a *whale*? What kind of life is this?" Yet, without this experience, we would never make it to Nineveh; without taking the complete journey to Nineveh, as this story will reveal, we would never know the true loving and compassionate nature of our God.

If, by the cover of this book, you were hoping for a "how to" manual about truck driving, this may not be for you. This book is not really about driving a "big truck"; it is simply the vehicle in which the lessons were taught to me and how I share it with you.

However, if you have ever felt lost in your life, I encourage you to continue to read, because this is a book about being "swallowed up" and finding the way out. It is about waking up, trapped, inside the belly of whatever your "whale" may be.

This book is written for you and me—the modern day Jonahs'.

Introduction

Discovering the hidden part of myself has taken me the entirety of my life to uncover. This excavating has been similar to an archeologist who searches, knowing that somewhere deep inside the earth lay a story that until now has been forgotten. Within me was buried such a story.

On the surface, I appeared to be everything I was trying to convey or personify. In the days of my youth, I studied the Bible and sought to find my value and purpose by pointing others to a god I only knew through paper and ink. This was a god of vengeance and wrath, a god who I only trusted through the interpretation of others. Serving such a god came at an enormous personal cost to me; I was suffocating under its cold, bitter, crushing weight. Like Adam and Eve I ran away naked and hid myself in the bushes, frightened, disillusioned.

Later, I attempted to seek my value and purpose through my educational pursuits—through degrees. I was unaware I had only traded the face of my "god" for that of my professors and the *experts*. In this, I had only changed the form and not my intent. It was the same old pain leading me, compelling me to search for my own acceptance, my own value by finding it through the experiences and definitions of others. During those years, I dutifully followed, even when I became aware the *experts* could be wrong. Having an education did not necessarily make someone a professional, nor did it mean that person knew how to respond to the complexities and challenges of life.

These years of my life could easily be summed up as the *searching years*—the longing years. Having lost all value for *secular* religion and education, I attempted to define myself repetitively by the varied occupations I'd held.

By my fortieth birthday, I was never more lost

than at that moment. I was living with my partner, Amanda. She had been my best friend for sixteen years and my loving spouse for nine years. We had two teenage sons, Matt and Seth, who were both attending their junior year of high school. I also shared my life with three dogs, two cats, a rabbit, a flock of chickens, and five young goats, all tucked away on five acres in Rockton, Illinois.

Though by the world's measurements I should have been ecstatically happy, I could not escape the feeling that I was *lost*, somehow, *adrift* in my life. It was as if I could hear a voice within calling to me. It always seemed to be there, arousing me from my sleep in the middle of the night; a nagging feeling that was ever present with me throughout my waking hours. Yet, for most of my life I did not trust this voice within me, because I refused to recognize it was God's voice asking me to go to Nineveh. I did not know it then, as I do now, that I was like Jonah, asleep in the bottom of the boat, utterly unaware that my life was completely off course, floating aimlessly among the waters of life on the path most traveled; the circular journey to Tarshish.

There I remained, repetitively broken, bleeding and hiding until the pain became too excruciating, too much to bear, that I decided to climb out of the murky waters and straight into the belly of the *whale*. In the pages that follow, you will find my story; however, it is not unique. What is unique is that I am willing to share it. I share it freely, with hope that we may all find our way to Nineveh.

With Love,
joyce cascio

*I know now,
there are many Jonahs' and joyces'
in the world.
Not all of us reside
in the belly of a "big fish" or "big truck."
I write this book for all of us;
in the hopes that we will
find the courage
to live our destines.*

The Zen of Trucking

The lobby was crowded with men carrying backpacks, only a few women scattered among the crowd. Some people were talking; most were just standing, careful not to make eye contact, looking down at the floor or staring into space. I could feel the apprehension in the room and it made me uncomfortable. I stood quietly alone, nervously wondering if I had made a mistake. Should I go back up stairs, retrieve my belongings and drive home before it became a costly financial mistake?

A woman's voice interrupted my thoughts, "The Paradise bus has arrived and is waiting in front of the hotel." I picked up my carrying bag and stepped into the line that was forming. We all filed quietly out the door. It was still dark outside and the air was harsh, chilling my exposed face and hands. We rode the twenty minute bus ride, mostly in silence. When we reached the school, we each stepped off the bus without being told, as if we had reverted back to our early childhood days. We followed the person in front of us into the classroom, found a seat, and waited to receive further instruction.

The first day we watched videos, listened to introductions, and at the end of the day, we were greeted by Mr. Paradise himself. He spoke passionately about the company, driving, and our future as drivers. As we left, we were instructed that tomorrow we would met our trainer and begin driving. From this point on, our advancement would be solely individual due to the extreme range of driving skills represented among the students. Some of my classmates had former truck driving experience, while others were not accustomed to shifting gears, having only driven cars with automatic transmissions. We were told our trainer would determine when we were ready to move into the next phase of our training.

On the bus ride back to our hotel that night, the level of anxiety had lessoned. There was conversation. People were smiling and laughing. There was anticipation for what laid ahead of us.

On the second day of training we were divided into groups of two and assigned to an instructor. I had been partnered with a tall quiet man named Terry. I immediately sensed his uncertainty about his decision to work for Paradise Trucking. His eyes and both corners of his mouth were cast down. I probably sensed his sadness because I was nursing my own. I sat down beside him and we gave each other a brief introduction while we waited for our instructor.

Terry confided to me that several months ago he had been laid off a job he had held for many years. Unable to find a job that would pay him a comparable income, he decided to try trucking. He had read the Paradise ads in his local newspaper, and having previous experience driving heavy equipment, he thought Paradise might be his answer. He told me he wasn't apprehensive about learning to drive. Rather, his concern was the time he would have to spend away from his wife, who was his high school sweetheart and best friend for more than 30 years.

While we were still getting acquainted, our instructor approached our table and introduced himself. His name was Edward Barns, a kind gentle man with thin graying hair, and I guessed him to be in his mid 40's. Like Terry, he was a devoted family man. He had two grown children from a previous marriage and a four year old son that had been a huge surprise to him and his current wife, because they had been told years earlier that she could not have children. They both counted their son a blessing and a gift. Whenever he spoke about either of them, there was a deep reverence and appreciation in his voice and facial expression. It wasn't a surprise when he told us that he liked to keep things simple, having only one requirement for passing a student: he must feel confident putting that student in a big truck on the same road as his wife and young son. If he could not in good conscience do this, he would not recommend that student's advancement.

When introductions were over, we went outside to the trucks. Since it would be our first day, we would only drive bobtail (without pulling a trailer). Terry drove in the morning, because I had forgotten my permit at the hotel. I knew myself well enough to recognize it was no accident that I had forgotten my permit. This was my first clue that I hadn't completely committed myself. I still harbored doubts, even though I had not been cognizant of it. Edward, however, was determined that nothing was going to stop me from driving on the first day. He instructed Terry to drive to the hotel so I could get my permit. On the way to the hotel it was obvious that Terry did have experience. He handled the truck with ease and a quiet confidence that left me in awe.

After lunch it was my opportunity to drive. I climbed up into the driver seat. I adjusted my seatbelt. I looked at the gages and stick shift. Edward nodded his head for me to begin. I pushed the clutch peddle in, turned the ignition key and started up the engine. I smiled at Edward, looked out through the windshield and then an all too familiar sensation began to take over my body. Heart pounding, legs shaking, I felt nauseous; I had butterflies in my stomach. I knew this wasn't just "nervousness"; it went so much deeper than that. It was the same terrorizing fear that had accompanied me throughout my entire life like an old lost friend, reappearing anytime I tried something new or tried to break away from old patterns.

"Ok, just take it slow. First, you'll just circle the lot in front of the school until you feel comfortable," Edward instructed me.

I slowly began to let out on the clutch, and just as the truck began to move I slammed my right foot hard on the brakes. We all lunged forward. I looked over at Edward.

"Ok, good. Let's try that again," he said never mentioning I nearly gave the three of us whiplash.

I again eased off the brakes, slowly released the clutch and right when we began to move, my right foot slammed down on the brakes, jerking us all forward once again. By now all the blood had drained from my face, and I sat wide eyed looking at Edward. He didn't say a word. He just motioned me onward.

Stop. Go. Stop. Go. I would continue to drive this way around the school lot, or "yard" as it is called. As I became more comfortable, the stopping and starting became further apart. Nevertheless, the rhythm of stopping and starting continued. Around and around the yard I drove.

Finally, Edward turned to me, "Ok, good. Now let's head out onto the road. Pull up to the stop sign and turn left," he said as casual as if I had been driving for years. At first I didn't say a word. I ignored him; but inside my head I was screaming, "Out onto the main road? Out into traffic! Is he insane? It is too soon to take me out into traffic!"

"Joyce, lets go," he said.

"Where?" I asked.

"Let's go out through the gate and turn left at the stop sign. We are going to have some fun now," he said smiling and rubbing his hands together in anticipation.

"Anticipation of his and our death," I thought to myself. "Edward, I don't think I am ready to go out there," I said challenging him to reconsider.

"Joyce, you are ready. So, let's go." His tone was not authoritative but direct, and I knew he was serious. "You can't be afraid of the truck. You must respect it, but you can't be afraid of it or you won't be able to drive it. Everyone is afraid at first. That is why we take students out right away so they can get past their fear. Now, let's go."

My hands now gripped the steering wheel tightly, and I turned left out onto the road in front of the school. Fortunately for me, it was approaching evening and Edward only had me drive around the block a couple times, and then we called it a day.

That night, back at my hotel room, I studied until I went to bed. The only time I stopped was to call home to talk with Amanda and the boys. The next morning I was up and ready early, so I could study until time to catch the bus. This would be the routine I would keep for the remaining 9 days of training.

The next day, Edward taught us how to hitch a trailer to our truck. After a couple of times around the yard, we were once again out onto the main road, learning how to take turns without taking down city street lights, stop signs, pedestrians, or other motorists.

On day four, Edward, still sensing my nervousness, decided to show me how much confidence he had in me. I quietly followed his instructions, turning when and where he instructed me. I was unaware that he was directing me onto an entrance ramp to the highway until I was on the merge lane. During the three previous days, I had not successfully taken the truck speed up to 55 mph. Now, I had no choice. The speed limit was 65 mph. I had to respond to the situation or get us all hurt or killed. Before I knew it, I was cruising down the highway at 60 mph.

"Well, don't look now, but I believe you are driving this truck," Edward said smiling.

When we arrived back to the school, Edward and Terry were both affirming about how well I was progressing with my driving. I, too, felt proud of my accomplishments. I returned that night to my room, and for the first time since I had arrived, believed I might be able to do this job.

Yet, each day when I awoke, it was as if the successes of the previous day had been stolen from me as I slept. I never said a word about my reluctance or my belief that I might not make it, or how each night I laid in bed with tears streaming down my face thinking I wanted to quit. It was as if Edward knew, and day after day he showed up as though he was my own personal Zen instructor, repeating the same mantras to me over and over: "Feel the truck!" "Stop thinking so much and just drive the truck!" "Get after it!" "Do it like you mean it!" "Have confidence in yourself!" "Stop fighting yourself!" "Don't worry about what other people think." And the big one, "You have to learn to let go of what just happened or it will multiply!!" I never responded to Edward's words. I didn't really know how to respond. His words both comforted and annoyed me. I thought to myself, "Am I that transparent that he can see through me?"

It came to a point where I thought that I only showed up, day after tiring day, to bite my lip, grind gears, drive grossly under the speed limit, forget the directions Edward told me and to constantly say, "I'm sorry," for all my mistakes.

On the tenth day of training I had been driving for about 30 minutes, still grinding gears; I was becoming frustrated with myself. I never said a word about feeling upset, but Edward kept telling me, "Let it go."

"Why does he keep telling me to let it go? He doesn't need to tell me to live in the present, I have been teaching people about living in the present for years," I said inwardly, defending myself against Edward's words.

While still analyzing these words in my head, I ran a stop sign. I was furious with myself. "How could I run a stop sign?" I scolded myself inwardly. I didn't say a word, but I grimaced, shook my head, and breathed a hard sigh.

"Let it go, Joyce," Edward warned. "You have to let things go or they become bigger. You can't hold onto every little mistake out here or you will hurt someone."

I didn't respond. I just kept my eyes facing forward, gritting my teeth, and drove straight ahead. Though I appeared to be aware of my surroundings, l clearly wasn't. A few moments later I approached a set of railroad tracks but failed to see the stop sign until I was about 10 feet in front of the tracks. Becoming panicked, I pressed hard on the brakes, and began frantically trying to down shift. In my panic, I was unable to find the correct gear. Up onto the train tracks my truck coasted in neutral, nearly coming to a stop, but the momentum pushed us slowly over before nearly stalling in the middle of the road. It was only then that I was able to shift back into gear. Edward didn't say a word as the next mile I grinded each gear repetitively before successfully shifting into it. I was clearly shaken and I didn't appear to be able to recover.

Finally, Edward spoke breaking the silence, "Joyce, pull over there."

I immediately pulled to the side of the road. "Ok. Now change places with me," he said. Once he was seated in the driver seat he drove us back to the school in silence. When we arrived back at the school, Edward turned off the truck and turned facing me. "Do you know what happened back there? I know, but I want to know if you know." He paused.

I didn't say a word.

"I was going to pass you today, even though normally tomorrow is the test day; you and Terry have both been doing so well, and I know how nervous you get. So, I was going to surprise you by doing your test today, without you knowing until it was over. But, after your performance today, I have no choice but to test you tomorrow," he said firmly. "Joyce, you are not going to be perfect. No one expects you to be perfect after ten days, but you expect it and you held onto running that stop sign and it multiplied into a bigger problem and it could have been serious."

I could tell he was disappointed. I was disappointed in myself. I felt foolish. Foolish for messing up, and foolish for thinking I could drive a big truck. I didn't really offer much in my defense. I was afraid if I spoke I would start to cry, so I sat quietly and listened to Edward repeat the same words to me again that he had been telling me throughout the training.

When I returned to my room that night I wanted to quit. I felt like a complete failure. I called Amanda to break the news to her that I might not make it through the program and that we may end up owing $3,700 for the training I had received. She was clearly disappointed too, but she stayed optimistic. She offered words of encouragement to me, as she often does.

"Honey, you can quit if you want to and everything will be ok. Don't worry. I just want you to be ok with your decision. I believe in you Joyce, and Edward believes in you too, but that's not the problem. *You* need to believe in you."

Even as I sat there and she spoke these words to me, I felt like I was in a bubble. I could hear the words, but I couldn't feel them. Later, when our conversation had ended, I felt comforted that I could quit and still have Amanda's support and love. Sitting there in the silence of my room I could feel the tug-a-war inside of myself, and for a moment I caught a glimpse of a larger lesson. All of this that I was experiencing had nothing to do with learning to drive a truck. Instead, this was a rare opportunity for me to become conscious of the fact that my driving was a reflection of the way I lived my life—timidly, hesitantly, fearfully, concerned about what others thought about me, and without awareness.

I was startled, even shocked at myself by this discovery, and that is when I knew I would pass the class. I had to pass, because now I knew there was so much more to lose than money. Reaching above me and turning off the light I asked myself, "How long have I been living my life in the shadows of my fears?" I waited for the answer.

The answer quietly came, "All of it."

The Comparison Game

During phase II of my training in Gary, Indiana, I learned I had several choices on the type of route I would drive. I could remain on the "dedicated" account for which I was hired, or I could select to be a solo or team driver on a "system" account.

The *dedicated* account I had been assigned was difficult for new drivers, often resulting in slow maneuvering accidents. This was mostly due to the advanced level of backing required for clearing cars, light posts, pedestrians, and other obstacles in the small parking lots where many of the stores were located. Many of the seasoned drivers did not want this job because dedicated accounts paid less money per mile. This account was unappealing to me because drivers had several stops a day, and must physically unload their own trucks. The product was usually loaded into boxes not weighing more than 30 lbs, but unloading 20,000 pounds of merchandise or more is a lot to require of someone who is also driving several hundred miles a day.

Nevertheless, the *dedicated* accounts were predictable, hauling the same freight for the same customer, often going to the same locations, and the miles were typical. This concentrated area allowed drivers on dedicated accounts to get home more frequently than *system* drivers.

A *system* driver is someone who has a great deal of change and flexibility in their routes. These drivers are placed into the *system* database, and then a computer will generate a load for that driver based on their availability and their location. Though it was computer generated, a trip planner could, and often did, make adjustments depending on the driver and the freight involved. A *system* driver often traveled all forty-eight states and into Canada, and was typically out 2 to 3 weeks before returning home. A driver's home time usually consisted of 1 day off for each week out.

For me, the advantages, to driving *system* outweighed the benefits for driving *dedicated*. Therefore, I decided I did not want the *dedicated* account to which I was assigned. That left me with two choices: I could go into the *system* either as a solo driver or as part of a team. Though I was extremely cautious and I had no accidents during any phase of my training, I lacked confidence. I still had difficulty shifting gears smoothly when driving through toll booths and measuring my distance through fuel islands; but the worst area for me was backing up. The idea of being on my own terrified me, and I did not believe I would be successful.

So, I decided to become a team driver, and was matched up with one of my classmates. His name was Brian, a young man about twenty-two years old who lived in the Chicago area, about 2 ½ hours away from my home. He was smart, witty, and one of the finest drivers in our class. He shifted perfectly and was not intimidated by backing into tight places as I was. Brian seemed infused with a confidence that was unshakable, even after he had a small backing accident during the third phase of our training program.

Based on my own fears and Brian's lack of fear, I felt he and I would be the perfect team. I sincerely enjoyed his company. In many ways, he reminded me of my youngest son, Seth, and Brian told me I reminded him of his mother. I guess we were both attempting to create a sense of family for our own security. Had we known what lay ahead of us, we may have chosen individuals who reminded us of different family members—those with whom we didn't have so many issues.

Brian and I decided he would park his car at my house while we were on the road together. The day before Brian and I left on our first load assignment, Brian met my entire family, and we invited him to stay the night in our home. The next morning, I excitedly hugged Amanda, Matt, and Seth goodbye. Then Brian and I climbed into our big truck and left for Reno, Nevada.

As the excitement of the first day passed, both Brian and I became easily agitated. For the first time, we became aware of how small a space we would be sharing, and neither of us was able to sleep while the other drove. I quickly recognized it was a trust issue for us, but that didn't help me to sleep. Finally, by late afternoon of day two, Brian was able to sleep soundly through the night for nearly ten hours while I drove. By day four, I hadn't slept more than a couple hours; I was a walking, driving zombie. Though Brian was sleeping more, he was exhausted too. He had a difficult time during the late night hours; several times he began to doze off behind the wheel. This only added to my paranoia about sleeping while someone else was driving. Although I was not accustomed to sleeping during the day and I was not a "night person," I began to drive the night shift, which only contributed to my sleep deprivation.

By day six, we had spent approximately one hundred and forty-four non-stop hours together and it began to take its toll. This is where Brian's confidence and my lack of confidence collided. I wanted to do everything by the book, and was vocal about any rule infractions. I became a representation of his nagging mother. Brian, being more of a free spirit, wanted to "wing it," becoming for me, the immature and irresponsible son. In short, we each wanted out. This would be our one and only trip as a team. I called our manager and asked her to assign us a load returning to Illinois so we could terminate this team agreement.

I would like to say that by day nine when we pulled into my driveway that Brian and I were still on good terms with one another, but we weren't. The truth is that we could no longer tolerate being together. Our final twenty-four hours had been the most difficult. I had reached my breaking point. I was going on eight days with nearly no sleep. I was delirious and my thoughts were incoherent. We both had many hurtful things to say to each other, but as Brian drove out of our driveway these were the only words I could remember him saying to me: "You are a stupid and negative person. All you do is talk about other people; putting other people down."

Over the course of nine days with Brian (that is two hundred and sixteen hours), we shared many conversations, but these are the only words I can recall with total clarity. Why these words? I knew why. These words struck a cord inside of me, but what cord? I knew that on some level I believed those particular words to be true for them to have impacted me so deeply.

"You are a stupid person" struck a nerve, but these words were not an earth shattering revelation. I was aware that this belief had haunted me for much of my life. I was amazed though, how subtly it continued to weave itself into the fabric of my life, remaining unnoticed by me that it was there, in so many of my daily decisions. Thinking on these words, I realized it was this old wound, a belief that I am inferior, not smart, or *stupid*, that had produced this teaming fiasco from the beginning. I had convinced myself that I needed someone else's input, even when that someone else was a novice like me. I had created a dependency on Brian because I was afraid I wasn't *smart enough* to figure out the right solutions by myself. Though I remembered him speaking these words to me, I did not feel hurt by them.

It was, however, his words, "You're so negative. All you do is talk about other people; putting other people down" that reverberated inside of me, shaking me to my foundation. I was confused, angered, and frustrated by these words, and that is why I knew I must uncover their meaning for me; I must understand them.

In the weeks that followed, I would replay those words repetitively in my mind, attempting to glean some substance from them. By now, I harbored no anger toward Brian. In fact, once I had a sound sleep, I returned to genuinely liking him again. I knew by then that my reactions to his words were not about him, but about me.

I tried to recall some of the conversations we had over the weeks since we met. Yes, it was true that I had discussed some of the instructors and had critiqued the program, but I did not mean the words I had spoken as a personal attack on anyone. It was also true that I had complained about how I believed the company had misrepresented itself during the hiring process. I did not mean any of the things I had said to be negative or hurtful. In general, I saw myself as kind, considerate and compassionate where most people were concerned.

To offer solace to myself, I began to go through a

list of people in my mind who knew me well. I thought about what they would say about me and my motives. I knew many of my coworkers and friends considered me a positive and loving person, with the best of intentions. I immediately felt vindicated. I decided to put the whole matter behind me and forget Brian's hurtful words as just an outburst of his anger. I sat smugly, basking in my vindication.

"Compared to whom?" a familiar voice from inside of me asked.

"Compared to whom?" I thought. "What does that mean?" I wondered silently, irritated.

"Compared to whom are you positive? Compared to whom do you not gossip or say negative things about others?" the voice asked softly, gently.

I sighed but remained quiet. I recognized this voice as my Higher Self. It is the Spirit, God, which dwells inside of me, and though I didn't want to understand this line of questioning—I did.

I understood that by comparing myself to others, I had fooled myself into believing I didn't share their behaviors. I had convinced myself that because I could point to others who seemed to talk about people with more frequency, and who were often more negative than me, that my words were harmless, even innocent.

In fact, as far as comparisons go, I had higher standards than most people I knew. How disillusioned I was to think that by comparing myself to others it somehow lessoned the toxicity of the poison seeping out of my words. In this moment,

I was being forced to face the truth; the *Comparison Game* was a lie.

My mind became a flood of questions and answers. "How many times during my lifetime have I played this game?" I wondered. After reflecting a moment, I realized it would be easier to count if I asked, "How many times in a day do I play the Comparison Game?"

"Do I play this game alone?" I asked myself. After a long pause, the answer came to me, "No, all of society is occupied with playing the comparison game. It is the foundation, the structural underpinnings of my society. It is how corporations determine their success, by comparing themselves to their competition. It is how students and schools are ranked, by comparing standardized tests and grades. The list is endless, comparing everything: movies, books, restaurants, neighborhoods, cars, occupations, relationships. . . ."

At that moment, I realized nothing in my life escaped this game. It is the method I used to determine the quality of my life. "Without the Comparison Game how would I know I am happy? How would anyone know?" I wondered. I recognized that the Comparison Game was how the collective "I's" gauged where "I's" are, and determined where "I's" are going. "How sad," I thought. The Comparison Game is a form of trickery, the slide of hand of a skillful magician which keeps me engaged in the world, but out of touch with me. I can't help but wonder, "What is the Comparison Game keeping me from knowing about myself?"

I was humbled by this experience. Brian hadn't been some random person recklessly passing through my life. He had been a messenger. Though Brain and I had not spoken since our last day together, I knew it was okay. I didn't need to feel sad about how things had gone with us. He delivered his message and with it he placed in my hand a priceless key. As I stood facing an endless row of doors, I knew this was only the beginning.

In the weeks and months ahead, I would need further lessons to help me discover to which door this key belonged. I was convinced, now more than ever, that a divine plan was unfolding in my life that had been set in motion by this big truck, and I knew it was a place I must go alone. The only thing I could do was to ride it out. So that is what I did every day; I rode the asphalt wave carrying me to the next adventure, my next lesson. . . .

Invisible

It is February and a blanket of snow stretches across the country. I am headed east across the Pennsylvania Turnpike to Philadelphia where it is reported that there is record snowfall. It is a beautiful sunny day, though temperatures remain in the single digits. The snow has mostly been removed from the highway, but patches of ice remain, making driving hazardous.

My CB radio is on, and I am listening to the chatter of other drivers. Some are complaining that the Paradise truck, that would be me, is slowing down traffic. I don't respond. It is true, the speed limit is 65 mph and I am only traveling 55 mph, but this is my first winter driving a big truck. I am in no hurry. I figure, if I am slowing anyone down, they can pass me, as I am in the right lane.

I notice in my mirror a car is fast approaching, passing numerous cars and trucks in the left lane. Ahead of me, I see a bridge. I look again into my driver side mirror. The car is gaining on me and will soon be in position to pass me. "I better slow down," I think to myself, deciding it would be better not to cross the bridge side by side. I immediately ease my right foot off the throttle and my truck begins to slow down 54, 53, 52, 50 mph.

"Damn it, Paradise!" I hear a driver yell at me over the CB.

"Must be a new driver, not used to driving in the snow," another chimes in.

The small grayish car passes me. There are two teenage girls in the car. I can see they are laughing and talking, and not aware that ice is on the bridge ahead. "They're going too fast; she will lose it on the bridge," I sense strongly within myself.

As the car reaches the bridge, it begins to swerve. I grab for my CB mic, "Backer down, eastside we have a wreck." I release the mic, letting it fall to the floor. I begin to bring my truck to a stop as I watch the car in front of me bounce off the concrete divider separating the east and west sides of the highway, and spin 360 degrees out of control before stopping facing north and south across my lane. Continuing to slow down, I could see the young driver, her mouth wide open as she watched this huge semi coming straight at her. It was difficult for me to gain traction because of the ice, but I remain calm and continue slowing down coming to a complete stop approximately 4 feet from the driver's door.

Fortunately, the two young women are only shaken. The damage to her car is minimal and they will live to tell about their adventure on the ice. Within minutes, the emergency road crew arrived and I am on my way. As I begin to drive away from the accident, on the west side of the road, on the same bridge, another accident has just taken place. A big truck and a car have collided. The big truck lay on its side sprawled out, blocking both lanes. A car, also on its side, appears to be missing its roof.

As I drive away from the scene of both accidents, my knees are shaking, my heart is pounding, and I feel nauseous. Over the CB, I hear drivers congratulating me for my excellent driving. They tell me it was a good thing that I had been leading the convoy in this instance. I thank them and drive onward. My hands are still trembling when I reach Philadelphia hours later.

Early the next morning I attempt to make my delivery, but the snow has been plowed so high that it is blocking most of the customer's narrow driveway. During the nearly 2 hour ordeal, one of the mud flaps on my truck had broken off by the pressure of the snow against the tire. Before proceeding on to my next assignment, I would need to have this replaced for safety reasons; it is against the law to drive a commercial vehicle without mud flaps. I placed a call into Paradise and I am instructed by the Safety Department as to where to take my truck for the repair.

Sitting at the repair shop waiting for my truck, I

decide to walk to the Subway® restaurant on the corner to have lunch. The repair shop faced an alley with the main street located at the back of the building. All exits and entrances faced the alley. From the alley, an old white house stood between the Subway® restaurant and the repair shop. After examining the situation, I realize that the only way to successfully arrive at Subway® is to walk through the alley, passing the white house. I can see two pitbull dogs, one white and one brown, playing in the yard. There is a fence separating the repair shop from the house, but there is no fence between the alley and the house. Walking in the alley, I would be exposed to the dogs.

"It isn't safe to walk across in front of those dogs," my intuition warns. "I'm an animal person. I love dogs and dogs love me. I don't need to be afraid," I said to myself, brushing off the warning. I can see the owner of the house, a large blonde haired woman in the front yard, cleaning out her white van just a few feet from where the dogs frolic. I am certain that if these dogs are dangerous, their owner would not keep them loose in a yard with no fence; with her so close by, surely there is no need for concern.

Walking through the parking lot toward the alley, I feel a strong current go thru my body: "I need to turn around," I think. Again, I ignore the warnings. Most of the truck stop Subway® restaurants do not carry the veggie-patty sandwich, my favorite one, and not having many opportunities to go to a non-truck stop Subway® in a big truck, I am not going to let this one pass me by. I shrug off my concern.

Casting caution to the wind, I take a step into the alley. At that moment, the two dogs that had previously been engrossed in play, suddenly stop and stare at me. "Hmm," I hesitate. "Maybe I should turn around," I think. The dogs do not move; they just stand there like they've turned to stone. I dismiss my uneasiness and proceed to walk through the alley.

All seems calm until I am in front of the house. Suddenly, for no apparent reason, both dogs charge at me growling. I freeze in place. As the dogs come closer, I yell, "Hey, hey, easy. Lady, your dogs!"

The woman begins yelling to her dogs. The white dog comes to a sliding stop once it reaches the alley, but the brown dog continues toward me. Jumping up it bites me in the center of my stomach, just an inch below my belly button. I feel the sting of the bite as it passes through my heavy jacket, sweat shirt, blouse, t-shirt and flannel lined jeans. I don't move.

The woman, now screaming at her dogs in a shrill voice, causes both dogs to turn toward her. I grab my stomach. I slowly begin to take a step. Then the brown dog that was just a few feet from me growls and attacks my left pant leg. The white dog joins in on this game, which I am certain they have played before: terrorizing the human. They pull me to the ground.

The woman is screaming, the dogs are snarling and pulling at my pant leg, and I am in complete and utter confusion. It is as if everything is moving in slow motion. Then, as suddenly as they began, the dogs let loose of my pant leg, turn and run back into their yard. The woman, saying nothing further, returns to cleaning her van. I drag myself upright and I slowly walk back to the repair shop, limping and holding my stomach.

My injuries are not serious. I have a bruised knee and a bruise on my stomach the size of a quarter, with welt imprints from the dog's teeth; thankfully the bite had not broken the skin. I walk around the remainder of the day in a state of disbelief, feeling sorry for myself that such a thing has happened to me.

Much later, I drive through the darkness of night, as hundreds of images pass through my mind. At 3:00 a.m. too tired and weary to travel further, I pull off the highway to rest. As I lay in my bunk, too exhausted to sleep, I replay the events of the past 24 hours in my mind. It all seems too familiar to be coincidental; somehow these two events are linked together. In both situations, I had sensed a potential problem. However, in one I had heeded the warning, while rejecting the warning of the other. I ask myself the following two questions over and over: "Why would I respond to the warning on the turnpike and not to the warning regarding the dogs? How are they different from one another?"

Laying there in the silence of the night, recalling numerous examples where I discounted warnings, I begin to see a pattern. The common denominator in all the examples is me. I can see the dramas of my life unfolding in that moment, and I realize that anytime I am given a warning in which others could be at risk, I respond to my internal alarm. However, when the risk is solely to me, I nearly always question, doubt, or completely ignore it. The near accident on the turnpike posed a potential harm to others, but the situation with the dogs threatened only me. The difference between the two became clear. I believed others matter, but that I do not.

This is painful for me, because I understand the intensity and destruction, of the hatred I am feeling toward myself. I esteem others more important, more worthy, and indispensable. I trust my inner voice when it comes to others because I recognize the sacred, the divine within them. However, I do not cherish my own sacredness. In fact, I reject it, believing myself to be insignificant.

For most of my life, I had longed to be someone different. I had even convinced myself that this was a godly trait. I told myself I was like Elisha who is mentioned in the Old Testament. Elisha was a young man who left his family, friends, and home, to follow an old prophet by the name of Elijah. What did Elisha hope to gain from following the prophet? He hoped to become like him, even an extension of him. When Elijah asked Elisha what he wanted in return for being in his service. Elisha responded with these words, "Please let a double portion of your [Elijah] spirit be upon me" (II Kings 2:9). Elisha is referenced from this point onward by his association to Elijah, and that it was Elijah's spirit that embodied or "rested on" him (II Kings 2:15).

Elisha seemed to disappear so Elijah's spirit could live on through him.

For years, I considered this story to reflect an admirable quality. I thought that seeking to be like someone who I thought honorable was *good*, humble, and noble. For hours, I labored to commit to memory thousands upon thousands of pieces of information from words, poems, and quotes that I regurgitated, never aware of the personal cost. I had learned early in my life that quoting others is considered by many to be an indication of one's level of education, versatility, mastery, and intelligence. I thought that by mimicking the words and actions of those I respected and honored that somehow, magically, their spirit might replace my own. I longed to be like Elisha, to wear the mantle of another, a disguise, to melt away from my own skin, to become other than who and what I was.

Of course, this never happened. Preferring others to myself had rendered me a hollow shell as I worked diligently to rid myself of me. I had forbidden myself to speak to me on my own behalf. In my own eyes, my life became void of meaning. I became invisible, as I struggled not to be seen for me, but for the identity of others. It was an insidious way of not being present in my own life; a rejection of my own personal power. Living within this framework, I would not need to seek my own counsel. I had something better, safer—the words and ideas of others that were considered "tried and true," to replace my own that I feared were not good enough.

At that moment, staring into the reality of my own pain, I realize that this is not responsible living. There is nothing honorable about reducing myself to a chameleon. My entire life had become one long sideshow of posturing, mimicking, and wearing disguises. I am not being *holy* or *humble* by denying my own existence and self worth. Nor can my worth be found in the world's description of me, because what is found outside of me can never define me. Definitions flow outward from their source, not inward.

This lesson is made clear to me; I understand it now. I do not need to become someone else, and I never did. I need only to express me. This is what I must do: I must awaken to my meaning, my purpose, which is my *life*. I must learn to participate in the world as I was intended. I must adequately join together with others, while maintaining my own full expression. I must do this if I am to find my way, if I am to find my voice, if I am to live as if I mattered.

Runaway Trains; Runaway Lives

Throughout my life, I have had only a surface understanding to what Jesus meant when he said, "He who has ears to hear, let him hear!" (Matt 11:15, Luke 8:8). Or when he said, "Having eyes, do you not see? Having ears, do you not hear?" (Mark 8:18). Today, the message in these words is unmistakably clear to me. These words are addressing the act of sleepwalking through life. These words are a call to conscious living. For years I had been teaching others about living consciously, while remaining profoundly unaware to how asleep I was in my own life.

As those first weeks and months passed behind the wheel, there were many times I drove aimlessly lost for hours. We had been told during class that this would happen, but as it continued to happen, I became frustrated and angry with myself, wondering, "How many times can one person become lost?" Yet, it was moments like these that I became aware of the places in my life where I was not only sleepwalking, but was completely catatonic.

For years I had said to myself and to others that I was, "directionally challenged." Looking back on it now, I understand that was my own defense mechanism giving me permission to hide the truth from myself. It wasn't that I had a *bad sense of direction* or that I was *unable to read a map* but that I simply did not pay attention. At first, I thought this was an abnormality unique to me, but as I continued trucking across the United States, how quickly that assumption faded; every day became an opportunity to learn that what I was experiencing was a very human condition.

One day while I was in North Carolina on my way to a shipper, my directions instructed me to turn left onto a residential road. Immediately upon turning onto the road, there was a warning sign, "No Trucks Ahead." I stopped. "How far ahead are trucks allowed to go?" I wondered to myself. The sign didn't say how far. I looked at my directions again. Maybe I had written them down wrong. But when I checked what I had written down with the directions from the computer, it was a match. Still sitting at a complete stop in the middle of my lane, I contemplated what to do next. To my right was a gas station on the corner. So, into the parking lot I went. Once inside, I greeted the cashier, a tall slender frail looking woman. I asked her for directions.

She replied with a heavy southern draw, "Oh, honey. I'm sorry I can't help you. I'm new to the area and I'm not sure. I've never heard of that place. So, I couldn't tell you if it is down that road or not."

"Well, do you know how far a truck can drive down this road?" I asked pointing to the road beside the gas station.

"No, but you can ask Joe, he might know."

I understood from her response that Joe must be a popular guy with the locals, and that she was not accustomed to having to point him out, but I wasn't a local. I was a stranger, a lost traveler, and I did not know Joe.

"Ahhhh, where can I find Joe?" I asked with a grin.

"He is over there at the grill. He has lived here his whole life and he knows the area real well. If anyone can help you he can," she said pointing toward a heavyset man at the grill.

I was relieved. "I appreciate the help," I said as I walked toward the grill where Joe stood. I waited my turn. "Hi, Joe. The cashier told me you might be able to help me." I told Joe my situation, just as I had told the cashier.

He looked at me and scratched his head. He looked at me again, this time shaking his head. He said, "No, I'm sorry, I've never heard of the place you're asking about. No, no never heard of that place you're asking about."

"Really?" I asked. I was completely puzzled. In a small southern town, I couldn't imagine anything as large as a warehouse getting by the locals, but in this case it seemed to have happened. I decided to ask for more clarity. "You are Joe, right? And you've lived here your whole life, right?"

"Yes, yes that is right. I'm Joe and I have lived here my whole life," he said proudly standing a little taller as he answered me. "But, I've never heard of the place you're asking about, and I don't know of any warehouses or big businesses down that road." He paused. "Sorry, I can't be more helpful."

I thanked them both for their help and before leaving, I decided to purchase a bottle of water. "So, you have just moved here to the area, huh?" I asked, making small talk with the cashier.

"Yeah, about two years ago."

"Oh, so did you just begin working here?"

"No, I have worked here since I moved here two years ago."

"Oh, okay," I said, trying not to appear shocked by her response. I resisted the urge to say, "Oh, you must not get out much." I realized that I was just annoyed. I decided to say nothing more; I just smiled and left.

Once outside, I asked another local if he was aware of any businesses on this road. He informed me that there was some kind of business about a block down the road but he wasn't certain the name. But he told me there was a big parking lot there where I could turn around if I was unable to find it. I started my truck, pulled out of the gas station and drove less than a 1/8 of a mile when I saw a sign with large letters with the name of the business I was trying to find.

I laughed to myself. I went inside to pick up my load, and joked with the guys that their business is the best kept secret in town, I told them my tale of being lost, and we all laughed.

A few days later, I was sitting for several hours at a customer located in North Lake, Illinois. When it came time to leave, I couldn't remember if I turned right or left when I entered. Pulling up to the gate, I stopped to ask the security guard, "Sir, which way do I need to turn to get back onto Highway 64?"

He looked at me with surprise. "Highway 64?" He paused. "I don't know where Highway 64 is. I don't think you can get on 64 from here," he said with a look of bewilderment.

"Really?" I said. Now I was the one bewildered because I was certain that Highway 64 was how I arrived at this location.

After a long pause he said, "Just ahead outside the gate, you can turn right and get onto Interstate 290. You can't miss it. There is a sign pointing to I-290 at the stop sign."

"Perfect. That is where I needed to end up anyway. Thanks for your help," I said and I drove out the gate. Upon reaching the stop sign, there was a sign pointing to I-290, just as he had said, and directly below it was a white highway sign with two black numbers. The two numbers were 64. I almost laughed. This man drives to work every day on Highway 64, but he doesn't know it as Highway 64. To him it is just the street he takes to get to work.

Day after day, I encountered people, like me, who

did not seem to have a clue where they were, or the name of the street or factory that existed one block away from where they lived. I couldn't help but wonder about these strange situations. It made me wonder about myself. How many times during my life have I thought I was traveling one road, only to discover later that I was on another road? The philosopher in me was intrigued, and I was content to ponder over these thoughts to amuse myself while driving. However, this lesson was not given to me to sit and ponder, but to take action in my life. What I have learned about Universal lessons over my lifetime is that they always repeat themselves, often with intensity, becoming more and more serious, until I understand them. This lesson was no different.

One afternoon in Wisconsin on Highway 41 N., I became lost once again. On this particular day, to my dismay, I found myself driving down a long, narrow, winding road with no place to turn around. I called the shipper, but heavy traffic flow made it impossible for me to stop; I needed both hands to drive, and could not hold the phone and drive at the same time, so I was on my own. I was elated when I could see I was approaching a "T" intersection that would bring me back out onto Highway 41.

My elation quickly turned to anxiety as I realized I would have to cross a double set of train tracks with a stop sign on the other side of the tracks before I could reach the road I needed. This type of railroad crossing creates a dangerous situation for big trucks because our length makes it impossible to completely clear the railroad tracks. It is illegal for any vehicle to stop on a railroad crossing.

I took a moment to assess my situation. Traffic was heavy in both directions. I waited. When the traffic began to slow, I decided to cross. As quickly as I began, a fast moving car approached speeding, tires squealing, making a left turn onto the same road where I sat, cutting me off so he could cross over the tracks. Immediately, I slammed on my brakes; fortunately for the driver I did not hit him. Unfortunately for me, my truck now straddled the tracks. More traffic followed. My palms began to sweat. Rubbing the moisture from my hands, I alternated them between the steering wheel and my pant legs. My mind became filled with images of scattered remains of a collided train and my big truck.

Suddenly, a terror takes hold in the pit of my stomach as I began to hear a train whistle in the distance. I hesitated to look, hoping I was mistaken, but the whistle continued to sound. I closed my eyes; turning my head to the left, slowly I opened them and then I saw it—the train approaching me as I sat on the tracks.

I looked to the road in front of me, right then left. Traffic was moving with intensity in front of me and around me. I was baffled by this. Could no one see this monstrosity of a truck sitting on the train tracks with a train moving toward it? I lifted my left foot off the clutch, allowing my truck to begin to move slowly forward, closer to the intersection. By now, I could hear my heartbeat pounding in my ears.

"What do I do?" I wondered to myself. "Should I get out and leave the truck? No, surely someone will let me out," I assured myself. I waited, but still the traffic did not slow or stop. I lunged forward in hopes traffic would be forced to stop; but I did not get far, because the flow of traffic was unaffected. I lifted my right foot from the throttle, slamming it hard against the brake just before I would have hit a motorist who quickly maneuvered left across my path passing over the tracks. This same motorist glared at me as he passed, clearly irritated with me for inconveniencing him.

By now the train was very near and should have been in clear view of anyone near this intersection. I heard its deep horn as it neared, drowning out all other sounds. Still, motorists continued dashing across the tracks, trying to beat the nearing train, prohibiting me from crossing. I was in full panic now. I began to scream out, "Stop! Stop! What is wrong with you people? Don't you see me? What the hell! Am I invisible or something?" I waved my hands as I screamed, but the traffic was not deterred. At this point I thought I was trapped in an old television episode of the Twilight Zone. "Could this be the end?" I thought to myself.

In those few short seconds, as I was sitting on those tracks, and the train was fast approaching me, my mind began to think about Amanda and the boys. I wondered what their lives would be like when I am gone. I wondered if they knew I loved them. I wondered if I had told them enough. I wished I could call them and tell them one more time. I wanted their voices to be the last I heard, but I could not. At that moment, we were lifetimes away from each other.

Suddenly, to my left a big truck pulled across both lanes of traffic, forcing the cars to stop. He blew his horn and motioned for me to cross the tracks. Shakily but quickly, I drove across the tracks. As I maneuvered onto the main road, I saw the train crossing where I had just been sitting. I waved to the driver in appreciation. I knew he saved my life, and he knew it too. As I drove away, I wondered if we were the only two who knew what happened there.

I pushed my right foot on the throttle. I had no time to waste, no time to reflect. I had to get to the shipper before their office closed. There was a shipment of fountains that I had to get to Georgia. So, I drove on to the shipper as if nothing happened. When I finally arrived, there was no discussion about my near death experience. He needed only my load number and my company name and then I was asked to back my trailer into a dock and to wait there until I was loaded.

An hour later, as I drove down side streets, over railroad tracks, and highways, it occurred to me the absurdity of my actions. I was nearly killed and I brushed it off as if this kind of an event happened to me everyday. My immediate response was to defend my actions, "I am a disciplined person, a professional. I had a job to do. I didn't have time to waste while I contemplated the world!" I recognized my defending ego voice. I waited for the understanding to come.

I knew I wasn't the only person who was living my life in oblivion. I realized many of the cars did not stop for me at that railroad crossing because they did not even see the train. In fact, judging by their blank expressions, many of them did not even see me. How could they miss something as large as a moving locomotive and a big truck? Simple—their minds were someplace else. They were not present in that moment; that moment did not truly exist for them. They were too caught up in what they were going to make for dinner, hurrying home to watch a soap opera, or to buy groceries, or worrying about the argument they had with a family member earlier that day, or too busy feeling hurt by what someone had said to them twenty years ago. It wasn't personal against me. For it to have been personal, I would have had to exist; but I did not exist—not to them.

To put this in better context for myself, I thought about the many times that while driving my car, I wouldn't notice a merging car until it nearly ran into me. Had I been in the moment, I would have noticed the road sign, or seen that the right or left lane was ending, forcing the other motorist into my lane. If I had been in the moment, I would have noticed the traffic light had turned red, and come to a controlled smooth stop; instead, I screeched to a halt, just inches from the other driver's bumper in front of me. I was responsible for committing the same acts as those drivers earlier. The big question was, "How often?" How often was I unaware of my surroundings? How often had I gone through the motions of my everyday life, completely callused to those around me, acting and thinking like I was the only person that mattered? How many times have I thought my needs and my presence were superior to those of others? Though, I did not want to admit it, I had committed variations of all these acts each day.

Yes, I had eyes and ears, but what was the quality of their functioning? Mostly, I was seeing and listening to the discords of my own life, and I only became acutely aware of another when it immediately impacted my personal sphere. I felt sadness. Not sadness in the form of guilt or shame, but in the form of an understanding, a compassion for the part of me that has believed I must remain separated in order to survive this life. I was experiencing my connective humanity. In that moment, I could sense in a tangible way the collective pain we all feel from living separate lives, and I had a foretaste of the beauty of our joining.

Life is about processes. I knew at the time, this lesson was not the final step, but a small shift or movement into a deeper awareness for me. For the time being, it would be enough to know that I was not *directionally challenged*. I could read a map well and I did not have to see myself as *lost*, even when the directions seemed to be *wrong*. Now, I was able to open my eyes and ears, soaking up all that surrounded me; I had become aware that the teacher was always near; a lesson was always being taught that had significance for me, and that was why I had been brought here.

Nowhere Land

It is 3:00 a.m. and I have just turned off Interstate 24 N. onto Highway 64 W. at Monteagle, Tennessee. Highway 64 is a scenic, but narrow, winding road. It is difficult to see because a thick fog hangs in the air like heavy white clouds. I am tired. My log book shows 10 ¾ hours for yesterday, with an eight hour break before beginning an hour ago, at 2:00 a.m. Actually, I worked 16 hours yesterday, and had less than a five hour break.

This is the norm: long days, short breaks, and the road. This has become my life. I have learned that in order to make on-time deliveries, I have to stretch my log book. This means that I log miles, and not the actual hours it takes me to get from one destination to the next. It may take me 3 hours or more to pass through the Chicago area, but I will only accrue 1 ½ hours on my log book. This provides me with an additional 1 ½ hours to drive. When stopping for a break, I will log 15 minutes off-duty instead of the actual 5 minutes. When I am at a customer's dock being loaded or unloaded, I will log-off duty regardless of the work activities I am required to perform. All of this is a way of extending my work day. This is against the laws that govern the trucking industry, but it is something that is encouraged and expected by the individual trucking companies.

It is a delicate balancing act. Most loads are time sensitive. If a driver is late for one of these loads, it can set a negative chain reaction into motion, resulting in additional expenses and loss of productivity: employees paid for standing around waiting, the customer being late on delivery commitments, the trucking company paying a fine for a late delivery, and so on and so forth.

This does not include the impact on the driver, the extra period he or she will be required to wait while other drivers who arrived on-time are unloaded or loaded first. It does not include the short mileage assignments that he or she will be given as a form of punishment for not being trustworthy to make on-time deliveries. Nor, does it include the friction created between the driver and his or her dispatcher. It is for these reasons, and so many more, that drivers will push themselves to the breaking point, and why the companies are willing to close their eyes to it: the more freight a driver moves, the more valuable and competitive the company becomes.

I turn onto Highway 431 N. and then onto State-Route 50. The fog has intensified; it has become a heavy blanket across the roads and fields. It is difficult to distinguish where the road begins and where it ends. The edges of the road border along creeks and hillsides. My speed is slow but steady; I am traveling approximately 40-45 mph. I am vigilant as I look for crossing animals, especially deer at this time of night. My eyes water from the strain and lack of sleep. I want so much to just close my eyes; my eyelids become heavy, my jaw relaxes, and my head drops forward.

I never know how long I drive this way before my body jerks me back into a slumberous, but conscious state. Regardless, it is an activity that has become too familiar. I shake my head, I roll the windows down, and I turn on the radio. I would pull over and get off the road, except the road has no shoulder, and with the fog I could become a hazard for other motorists. I keep pushing myself. I do a lot of self-talk on these types of trips, "Stay awake! You can do it!! Not much longer!" My body becomes heavy and every movement is a laborious effort.

As the first rays of morning's light begin to streak across the sky I arrive at my destination just outside of Lewisburg, Tennessee. There isn't another driver in sight; it is just me and the security guard on the premises. The security guard is a rather large grey haired man with a fragile disposition. His shoulders and chest lean slightly forward and he walks with a limp. I pull up to the gate and stop.

"You need to slide your tandems (my back trailer tires) all the way to the back, please," he said without making eye contact with me. This is a common request because it makes the loading safer for certain types of loading docks. On newer trailers, pulling the tandem locking pins is easy, nearly no strength needed; however, the older model trailers are extremely difficult to pull loose. "Okay," I say politely, but inwardly I am frustrated. I have an older model trailer. I exit my truck, walk to the end of my trailer on the left side. I squat down looking up under my trailer. I can see that my pin is not centered, but I reach in, taking hold of the bar and pull. It will not budge. I look back at the security guard who is still standing in the same place, clip board in hand, watching me. I smile and walk back to the front of my truck.

"I have to get the pin to center so I can pull the bar," I say climbing into my truck. He nods. I put my truck into gear and rock my trailer slightly. I exit the truck again. Walking to the back of the truck I attempt again to pull the bar, but it will not dislodge. I walk back to the front of my truck and climb into my cab, repeating the same steps as before. I continue this process over and over for ten minutes. By now, the security guard has moved back inside.

I go inside to ask for his help. He is eating his breakfast—a large plate of barbeque chicken, mashed potatoes with gravy, and bread. As he looks up at me, there is barbeque sauce and butter spread across his face.

"I am sorry to bother you, but I am having some trouble getting my tandems to release. Could you help me?"

"Oh, no, I can't help you. I am disabled and I am unable to do anything physical," he says still engrossed in his chicken delight. "I have a hammer, so you can hammer the pins," he adds quickly, glancing up, before returning to his meal.

"No, I have a hammer. I will just keep trying. Thanks."

Walking back out to my truck, I feel frustrated. It takes me another 20 minutes before I am able to get the pins to release.

After sliding my tandems and successfully dropping my empty trailer in its parking spot, I search for the loaded trailer I am to pick up. Upon finding my trailer, I inspect and hook to it quickly. Knowing that it will violate bridge laws to drive with my back tires at the end of my trailer, I attempt to slide my tandems forward. However, a bend in the middle of the release bar combined with the weight of the load makes it difficult for me to pull the bar out.

Back and forth, in and out of my truck I climb for over an hour. I pull and hammer, and hammer and pull. Water, which has melted from the snow, covers the pavement where the trailers are parked. My knees are wet from kneeling down and crawling under my trailer. By now, I am angry. My mind is racing. "I'd like to light a match under this trailer," I think to myself. I have worked myself into a frenzy. I pull wildly at the bar. I slam the hammer hard against the pins. Small chips of metal and paint flaked off, but the pins do not go in far enough to slide.

"Oh God," I scream out in anger, collapsing, falling backward to the ground beside the trailer. I just lay there. I feel the water underneath me as it seeps into my clothes and the back of my head, drenching my hair. I do not care. I do not move. I am cold, exhausted, and hungry. I want nothing more than to quit this job; to escape this hell I have created for myself.

"I can't do this anymore!" I scream. "I've had it, enough of this madness!"

I remain on the ground. My body is becoming numb by the ice water I am laying in; I am not sure if I am awake or asleep.

"Are you okay?" a voice yells to me.

Still lying on the ground, I roll my head to the left. It is the security guard. "Hmm, he must be done eating his breakfast," I think to myself. I slowly get up. "Yeah, I am fine," I say firmly.

"Are you sure?"

"Yes, I'm sure," I say annoyed.

"You scared me lying there. I thought you had gotten hurt or something."

"No, I am just resting. I am having trouble

sliding my tandems again."

"Oh, okay. I have to get back inside the office because I am the only one here," he says as he drives away.

I resume my fight with the trailer. I pull wildly, yanking, jerking; anything to get this bar to move, but it will not budge. I cry. I began to yell at the trailer and into the air, "You stupid piece of shit!! God, I hate this job!! I want to quit!! I am going to quit!!! Right now, I am going to quit!! I don't care about the $3,700.00 anymore. If Amanda doesn't want me because of the added debt, then so what, I don't care anymore!"

These words barely leave my lips when I begin to look around me. Where would I go? "I am in the middle of nowhere," I tell myself. "How could I get home from here? There isn't an airport, bus station, taxi anywhere near here. I am stuck! I have no choice but to drive this piece of shit out of here. It is the only way out of this, god forsaken, hell hole."

Then I have a sobering moment. "Interesting choice of words," I say to myself. Then I think, "It isn't possible for me to be in the middle of nowhere. There is ground beneath my feet and it is obviously somewhere to all the people who live, play, work, and die here. It is only a nowhere land to me."

I find it outrageous that in the middle of this parking lot, surrounded by trailers, with my backside soaking wet, and now running behind on my schedule, that I can take the time to be philosophical. "This is ridiculous!" I say in my defense, "It is just an expression. Lots of people say it about being out in the country." But I can not shake the emotions these words speak to me.

I turn and lean against my truck. "Nowhere Land?" I ask as a question. "Out in the middle of nowhere," I say out loud, and let my voice trail off as I delve deeper into thought. I wonder, "How many times have I been **somewhere,** only to think I was *nowhere,* and that it did not matter or that it was not important?" I knew the answer is more times than I can count.

I pause, "Nowhere Land is where people go when they have no sense of self. Being in Nowhere Land is like walking in the land of the lost." Sadly, still leaning against the trailer, I realize I do not need to go far to reach home, I am home. "Nowhere Land is where I live; it is where I've taken residence most of my life," I say to myself. I begin to walk around my big truck, picking up my scattered tools.

I climb back into my truck and pull slowly out from between the two trailers on either side of me. I park near the front gate and decide to wait until another driver enters so I can ask for assistance.

Shortly, thereafter, a driver arrives. I flag him down and asked him to assist me with pulling my tandems. About 15 minutes later, I drive out of the gate leaving Lewisburg, Tennessee behind me. "What keeps people stuck in Nowhere Land?" I ask myself. After a few moments the words come, "Being blinded by their anger, they are unable to see their way out."

A few hours later, I stop to rest at a truck stop and to buy some water. While inside the store, I think about Jonah. To me, Jonah is the classic character of being lost; he allowed his anger to keep him from his life's purpose. I think about how many times throughout my life I have identified with Jonah. Somehow, like Jonah, I never seem to make it to Nineveh. Walking back out to my big truck, I stop about 100 feet from it. I am stunned by what I see in front of me. "My truck is my whale," I say to myself. "I don't just feel like Jonah; I am experiencing Jonah." From this moment, I become aware I am in the *belly of the big truck*.

I recognize that Jonah's *whale* and my *big truck* are both representations of being confined, trapped, closed-off, and swallowed up. It is then that I realize that if I can figure out Jonah's conflict, I might find insights about myself.

After some thought, I listed 4 main issues:

Jonah had decided that the task God asked of him was meaningless; that it didn't matter.

Jonah had closed his heart because of his traditions and beliefs.

Jonah was angry because of his inability to control the outcome.

Jonah had a warped sense of justice.

I had believed my entire life that Jonah's problems stemmed from not going to Nineveh. In actuality, it wasn't about Nineveh at all. Jonah's issues had to do with his closed heart; a heart he had closed long before his *whale* appeared and swallowed him up. It was Jonah's closed heart that placed him out in the middle of the ocean, adrift among the waves. Jonah was in *Nowhere Land*. Jonah had lost his way, and surely would have drowned in the ocean. The big fish, the *whale*, wasn't his punishment; it was his lifeboat.

War
Enemies
Envy
Fear
Oppression
Violence
Malice
Hate
Survival
Mistrust
Consumption
Greed

Copyright Charles Hackworth © 2004

Weapons of Mass Destruction

I am headed west to Tucson, Arizona. I am relieved this load will take me several days to drive, because I have had more than my share of "short loads" (loads with only 300-400 miles). Short loads are more difficult, usually delivering the same day or within 24 hours of the scheduled pickup time. Often the trailers are not preloaded, causing me delays. Even when the trailers are preloaded, there is the time it takes me to get checked into and out of a shipper's yard, and how long that will take depends on each shipper. Then I must rush, rush, rush, to the customer to make an on-time delivery. Once I deliver the load, there is the added annoyance of having to locate another empty trailer, which may require having to drive additional miles to find. Yes, the "long haul" loads, the ones with 800 miles or more, are the ones I most prefer. My work day is still 14-17 hours, but long hours driving are easier than the physical labor and hassles involved with the shorter hauls.

As I drive across the country, I think about many things; generally these days it is the "War-on-Terrorism" that America is waging against Iraq that is in the forefront of my mind. The thought of *this* war or *any* war disturbs me, because I do not understand the rationale behind war. For me, war has never seemed a viable solution; I know war will never bring peace. It may bring a pause to a conflict, but a "pause" is not peace. It is merely a time for re-grouping, re-strategizing, re-aligning; but it is not peace. For today, I remain among the minority who hold this opinion.

I want to forget the war, to block it out somehow, but it seems impossible. Though I am thousands of miles away from the battle field, I feel trapped inside of it; the war appears to surround me. I can hear the beating battle drums of war at the truck stops, the stores, and the places I make my deliveries. Everywhere I go, it is the prominent topic of angry discussion.

These days, I drive with the radio off. I find it exhausting listening to the endless rhetoric about the war, and to the continuous replaying of new and old songs that have been written to support, give tribute to, or justify war. I have come to view all of this as a subtle form of brainwashing, inducing mindless support on behalf of an unjust war.

Even when I turn on my CB radio, the war is there. The few drivers who are brave enough to voice their opposition to the war are verbally assaulted and threatened with bodily harm. Angry drivers provide explicit and descriptive acts of violence ranging from beatings with baseball bats or crow bars to sodomy. It is some of the ugliest and most vile talk I have ever heard, and when I hear it, my stomach twists and turns. It makes me nauseous, because I *feel* the hatred growing; I sense the deep seated fear that is poisoning the airwaves, and I see it consuming those I meet daily. All of this leaves me saddened, and I am fearful about where all this hatred is leading.

Having no place to escape it leaves me overwhelmed and worn out, but when I stop to rest at night I find it difficult to sleep. I toss and turn in my bunk until daylight, and then I begin my day anew, repeating the events from the day before. Tonight, I decide to do something different. Instead of tossing and turning in my bunk, I take out a pen and paper and I write these unsettling words. . . .

Feed Me another Spoonful of Hatred

Tell me how I should dress,
  What I should wear.
    What styles are in and which are out.
      What I should do.
        What I should earn.
          What I should drive.
            What house I should live in. . . .
              And I will drink it up.

Tell me to have no thoughts,
    Except those I am given
        But convince me
            these thoughts are my own.
           Because I need to know
            I am unique, *special*.

                Feed me another spoonful
                of this self hate
                    And I will drink it up.

Go ahead
    Feed me
        You have my attention now.

Tell me the rest of the world is evil
    Tell me to fear those unlike you and me.

Tell me *sometimes* killing
    in the name of god
        Is necessary for our survival

And I will place my lips
    upon this bitter cup
        And I will swallow;
            not as the poison it is,
                But as a bitter medicine
                    Only the brave can bear.

Weapons of Mass Destruction

Tell me it isn't hatred
  We only engage in "just" wars
    And civilian causalities
      Are an unfortunate event
        in times like these.

And I will close my eyes.
  I will close my eyes
    to the broken, bleeding,
      Charred, mangled bodies
        of women, children, and
          Men lying face down
            in the streets.

Tell me it isn't hatred
  That makes us
    gather round our televisions at night
      Daring to observe these images
        on the evening news
          As if it were a festival of lights
            And not the stench of death
              lying under the rubble
                Of fallen walls
                    Made of concrete and stone.

Tell me none of this is hatred
   or Colonization
      But "Nation Building"
         So the bitter medicine
            can become more palatable

            So can I drink
               believing we
                  are admirable
                     We are heroes.

Tell me weapons of mass destruction are safe
   In the right hands—*OURS*

Tell me all these things and more
   And I will drink and drink and drink
      Until I bloat and become too numb to stop

   I will drink and drink and drink
      Until I am drunken by the lies
         I have swallowed up
            and the lies that I have lived.

      I will drink and drink
         until I can drink
            No more.

And lying there
  In my delirium
    My only regret is
      that I could not drink more

Unaware
    that my own destruction is at hand
      I close my eyes
        and still craving the bitter drink
          The Earth swallows me up
            And I am no more.

When I am finished writing I lay my pen aside and study these phrases. At the time I was writing it, I felt I was venting about my society. However, after rereading it, I find these words to be more intimate than general. No, this is something more; it is personal, a message I am writing to myself. I read these words again slowly, digesting each word, each sentence. It is only then that I understand that these words are attempting to convey to me a deeper meaning about the war. To my surprise, I, too am being consumed by my own form of hatred.

"But how? How can I be consumed by hatred?" I thought to myself. "I am a pacifist."

"That is true, but being a pacifist is hardly an inoculation against hatred, only against murder or physical violence," my soul answered me.

I found this thought particularly troubling.

Though I did not want to accept any responsibility for the war, somewhere inside of me, I knew I was just as *involved*, just as *responsible*, and just as *hateful* as those I disdained for supporting the war or those drivers I heard on the radio. It was late, my body was weary, and I needed to rest. I decided to dismiss these thoughts, and I drifted off to sleep.

The following two days were more of the same. Waking up around 5:00 a.m. and driving until 9:00-10:00 p.m. with only a few stops for fueling and restroom breaks to interrupt the monotony. Still not willing to explore the possibility of my own involvement in the war, I concentrated my energies and thoughts on my excitement about going back to the desert and visiting my mother and brother who lived in Tucson.

It had been more than 4 years since Amanda, the boys, and I had moved away from Arizona, and this would be my first return trip to Tucson. Prior to leaving Arizona, I had been satisfied with the relationship I had with my mother. Over the years she and I had healed many wounds between us, and we had managed to create a relationship where a strained and difficult one had existed before.

Through the years we had many issues to contend with. In my earlier years, my mother disapproved of my being a lesbian. It was not easy for her to understand how her daughter could be so bold as to live her life without a man. During those years, I often loathed my mother for thinking she needed a man so desperately, that she would settle for someone I believed was not worthy of her. As time passed, my mother learned to accept that I was never going to need a man, not the way she did; and I came to accept that she would probably always need one in hers.

It was this mutual acceptance that had made the holidays and family visits more enjoyable. She became an important part of Seth's life, and she even attended our Holy Union, when Amanda and I were married. Whenever we came to visit, she always welcomed Amanda, and she referred to Matt as her grandson, too.

On the surface, things appeared to be well between us, but there still remained an awkwardness, an uneasiness that I had not been willing to resolve. Often times I visited her because I felt obligated; it was a holiday, or birthday or it had been months since I had seen or talked with her. When we visited, time seemed to stand still. I recalled on several occasions thinking it must be time to go, only to realize we had barely been there an hour. Somehow I had convinced myself that it was easier to have this type of relationship with my mother than to invest the time and energy into dealing with the real issues that still separated us. I even went as far as to convince myself that my behavior was noble, generous, kind, and most of all, loving. I told myself all these lies, while unconsciously, my bitterness and anger ate away at me like a cancerous sore.

Life is an interesting teacher, having many ironies. One such irony was that as my children grew older, into teenagers, I often found it interesting how differently we remembered the same events. At first, I held a firm belief that there was a *right* and *wrong* way for remembering the past. That is, if the recollections were not identical, someone had to be *lying*. However, with the passing of time, I came to realize that no one was lying; we were only looking through different filters. It took my relationship with my sons to teach me that each of us, based on our own perceptions, experiences, and understandings, were actually experiencing the world differently, which consequently led to different conclusions. Having this realization, I began to question my personal objectivity, my reality. In the end, I concluded that my accuracy was tainted. Everything that I believed was merely a reflection of what I *wanted* to believe; therefore it was subjective, and not fully trustworthy.

Having this insight, I began to question my relationship with my mother. I learned that what plagued my relationship with her had more to do with *my* perceptions than any other reasons. As I began to take responsibility for the awkwardness I felt around my mother, I was able to see through the looking glass more clearly.

The relationship I experienced with my mother had been my own creation and no one else's. What I had been calling *Truth* was a false reality, a misperception. At first, this was difficult for me to digest. As far back as I could remember, I had always believed my mother was ashamed of me, did not love me, and never wanted me. I was the self proclaimed black sheep of my family, believing that everyone else was loved in my family except me. I had grown up convinced that my mother was "uninterested" in my life. I had a long list in my mind of band and choir performances, school plays, sporting events, etc. that my mother never attended. I had held onto this list my entire life, and I visited it regularly as a way of holding her accountable and for justifying my indifference toward her.

As the years passed, I found myself repetitively watching for any clues to support my position. I would be infuriated when my mother would call me on the phone to remind me of one of my brothers' or sister's birthday, and then later during that same year she would forget to call me on mine. I felt equally upset when she would brag about the accomplishments of one of my siblings when she so rarely seemed to acknowledge mine.

It was difficult after so many years to ask myself to consider other possibilities for my mother's actions. My revelations did not come quickly. Instead, they came in waves, bits and pieces of small conversations I had with my mother over the telephone since I had moved away. Finally, one day it all made sense. I began to understand my mother and to realize how wrong I had been about her. Listening to the things she said and the things she did not say, I came to understand all I needed to know for my healing. She had not been some monster rejecting me. She had been fighting her own inner demons that had nothing to do with me or my sister or brothers.

Living in a small town, there are few secrets, and

Belpre, Ohio was no different. My mother's life read like a "made for T.V. movie" for many of the people there. We lived in a town where most people attended church every Sunday and remained married for life, regardless of their marital unhappiness. In such a town, my mother's life went against the grain. She was a several time divorcee with limited education and young children. She had held many jobs in her early years, usually bartending and dancing in topless establishments where she had been on an endless quest for a new husband and father for her children.

 I remembered times when my mother made what I had thought were irrelevant comments. Her common response was, "I don't want to see those people," when explaining her reasons for not attending my school functions. I could never understand what "people" she was referring to. At the time I was unaware of social politics and the imbalance of power my mother experienced. The power my mother had experienced working inside of the local clubs did not translate to her life on the outside. She was uncomfortable in social situations, because she feared seeing those same men with whom she had a personal history sitting with their wives. My mother feared public humiliation being branded the woman with the scarlet letter. She lived day to day, haunted by the possible confrontation with a past I knew little or nothing about, because I lacked the life experience to understand.

 All my life I had missed this vital piece. I had

been so consumed with my own thoughts about her rejecting me that I had failed to recognize that she did not attend any of my siblings' school functions either. As I grew older, I was so caught up in my obsession to find additional clues at the scene of her crimes that I had been unwilling to acknowledge that my mother, at one time or another had forgotten all of our birthdays. Nor had I been willing to acknowledge the fact that my mother discussed my accomplishments with my other siblings, just as she had discussed theirs with me.

    Choosing to see things from a different perspective caused me to identify the gap that existed between our perceptions. I had not been witnessing a rejection of me, but of my mother's own self rejection. What I had perceived as her rejection of me was a mistake; it had nothing to do with me. Nevertheless, I had rejected her in retaliation for what I had interpreted as her rejection of me. The awkwardness I had felt with my mother all those years was from my harboring a deep resentment toward what I perceived to be an imperfect mother and my lost childhood. I did this while I remained blinded to the pain and the literal wreckage it was creating in my life.

    This trip to Tucson would be the first time I would see my mother face to face since I experienced this revelation. Though we had been talking daily on the telephone for months, I knew that a telephone call could not capture all the emotions and subtleties in a face to face meeting. I knew this would be a monumental moment in our relationship, and I hoped for the best.

I arrived in Tucson around 8:00 p.m. on a Thursday night. The sun was still shinning when I drove up to my mother's boyfriend's house where my mother had been living for the past two years. She and her boyfriend were waiting, standing out in the front yard, waving to me.

As I stepped out of my truck and onto the desert sand, my mother was already at my side with her arms wide open. She hugged me tightly. She looked so much older now, resembling my grandmother. When I hugged her she felt frail and her skin was soft, thin like an elderly person's. I was experiencing for the first time the reality that even my mother, like all things of this world, was growing old. I was stunned. She had always been so wild and carefree that somehow it never occurred to me that she, too, would age. It scared me to see her that way.

I grabbed my overnight bag and went into the house with them. My brother Charlie arrived soon afterwards. To my surprise my mother had made me a vegetarian meal with homemade bread. I did not dare tell her I no longer ate bread because it gave me digestive problems and that it contained too many carbohydrates. No, instead, I sat down and I ate the dinner that she had lovingly prepared for me. That evening the three of us talked through most of the night.

The next morning I made my delivery early, and to my delight my next load was going to Missouri with a Tuesday delivery date. I knew there was plenty of time to deliver it, so I decided to remain with my mother through the weekend. During that weekend, I had time alone with my brother, Charlie. I found myself amazed by the changes I saw in him. Like my mother, he also had aged, grown calmer, mellowed. Yet, there was a sadness, even a loneliness I sensed about him that made me hurt for him. He took me to his apartment and he shared with me his most recent artwork. I enjoyed our talks about his dreams, his work, and his ability to express the beauty and sadness he saw everywhere. I found myself moved by his art: the depth, the intensity, and the insights I experienced by looking at them. Though he doubted himself, because he had no formal training or education regarding art, I did not. I could see in him what I had always seen—a true artist. I encouraged him to continue to hone his skills and to never give up on his dreams. I had never realized before this trip how much Charlie still valued my opinion; after all these years, he still looked up to his big sister. Spending time with him made me realize how much I had missed him.

Early that Sunday, as I hugged them goodbye, a part of me did not want to leave. I wanted to stay, to talk, to laugh, to be near my mother and my brother. I knew I must leave, and that by leaving it would bring me one step closer to returning home to Amanda and the boys, but that did not stop the tears I cried as I drove away. The child's heart inside of me did not want to go. It was at that moment that I understood that I had never outgrown my need for my family; indeed, nobody ever does.

As I drove away that morning, I felt lighter in my spirit. Gone were the hurtful years of my youth. Gone were the hateful words that had been spoken. Gone were the years of lonely nights I had cried, thinking that my mother never loved me; now I knew she did. I was no black sheep and I had never been one. My mother did love me, and she always had. I was completely at peace with my mother. This was a miraculous moment, because nothing had changed except my perception.

As I drove in silence to Missouri and on to Illinois, I thought about how much pain one misjudgment, one misperception had caused me, and how many years I had carried it through my life. Like a disease that slowly eats away the body, my misperceptions had eaten away at my life. I realized how subjective my memories were, and how fragile the histories were that I had constructed from them, and I wondered, "Were there others? Other misperceptions? Other false histories I had constructed and allowed to consume my life?"

I knew the answer was "yes". After a short pause, I asked myself, "How many? How many other petty wars am I wagging in my life with the sources of those conflicts just as fictitious as the one that existed between my mother and I?"

Inwardly, I knew the answer was hundreds, possibly even thousands. I was startled and frustrated by this. "I have that many conflicts? I am involved in that many wars? Who am I fighting?" I questioned.

Sadly, the truth was all around me. I was fighting everyone, including myself. I was engaged in conflict daily. All I had to do was recall most of my daily interactions with my dispatcher, or the clerks at the warehouses where I made my pickups or deliveries. Yet, my conflict did not end there. I was in conflict about driving my big truck. On the weekends that I returned home, I was in conflict with my sons, or with Amanda about our sons. I was in conflict with innate objects as well: the traffic, a dock that was difficult to back into, or the value of money and the power it wielded over my life. My entire existence seemed to be one huge continuous strand of conflict; I was caught-up in a persistent state of warring.

"How can this be? Where did I go wrong?" I questioned. "Rarely do I raise my voice! Rarely, do I become argumentative! Rarely, am I unkind or rude to another, regardless of their treatment toward me! In fact, the only person I know that can rattle me is my youngest son, Seth. Otherwise, I am a walking billboard of harmony," I said, these words hoping to convince myself that *Harmony* was my middle name instead of *Warrior*.

I knew this was futile reasoning. I was only referring to the outward manifestation of hostility, which was no indicator of the conflict ragging inside of me. It was obvious to me that I had mistaken silence as harmony and not for the conflict it was. "No wonder peace has eluded me," I thought. This was a poignant moment for me, because it was the first time I accepted the severity, the far reaching arm of conflict in my life. "What is the root of my conflict, my thirst for war?" I asked.

"My own fear turned into hate," my inner voice answered.

At first, I wanted to reject this notion, this reasoning. Yet, as I began to list the conflicts that came to my mind in all of them, I could see my fears. My fear of loss: my fear of losing my job, losing my relationships, losing my life. . . . "Ok. The fear I agree with, but not with the hatred," I said, still not grasping the deep impact of my fear. I waited. "Ok. Maybe I do hate my job, but not my dispatcher, not the clerk at the shipping yards, not my children, not my friends, not Amanda, not my life!" I said emphatically.

As I continued to drive, I thought about the pain behind the emotion of loss. I concluded that my fear of loss *was* about losing something or someone. "It is not like I can misplace my job, someone, or something," I said. Yet, as quickly as I said it, I understood the word *loss* could easily be replaced with the word *take*.

"My fear is that someone will *take* something or someone from me. I fear the emptiness the *taking* will leave behind. I fear the hurt, the pain that I will experience emotionally, mentally, economically, or physically as a result of that *loss*, that *taking*," I thought to myself.

At that moment, I understood that my conflict represented my defense; it was my protector. Fear became hate in my moments of desperation, when I was willing to do or say anything to regain what I believed was being taken or lost from me. "Therefore, it is true; all conflict is the result of a deeply embedded hate. The conflict is merely the physical manifestation that the hate exists," I thought to myself.

It was shocking for me to learn that I had spent my entire life running after an illusion of peace. For me, Peace, had been about maintaining, keeping the things I wanted in my life. In this, peace was not peace at all, but a struggle: grasping, holding, clinging, fighting, and warring.

As much as I did not want it to be true, I knew I had traded the reality of Peace for an illusion of safety. On an unconscious level, I had believed in the qualities of aggression, conflict, and warring to keep me safe. Though I had spent most of my life pursuing peace, I feared it. I feared what peace might cost me when resolving conflicts, and there was little I was willing to give up. I had to admit to myself that as much as I wanted peace, I was caught in a vicious cycle of continuously teaching and re-teaching the basic lesson of human survival—survival at any cost. In truth, the idea of a peaceful world without the use of coercion did not exist for me. I had to admit, just like the political leaders of the world, that I believed a show of force, and not my extension of Peace, secured my safety in the world.

Suddenly, it did not seem to matter where wars were fought, whether in my living room or on the distant shores of some far away country. All conflict had the same agenda—to validate hatred. In all of this, I understood that *War* has many faces and

Terrorism wears many disguises. Before one unkind word could ever be spoken, or one blow ever thrown, or hand-to-hand combat engaged, before one bomb could be dropped, or one gun fired—war already existed. The violence was the outward manifestation, the expression, or the final stages in a tribute to that war. It became clear to me that the greatest weapon of mass destruction would never be found in a laboratory, or military post, but in some darkened corner of the hardened, unhealed, human heart.

As I pulled into my driveway, I did so with the knowledge that it is Peace, not war, that stands knocking at the door of my heart. I had always thought it was the other way around. That I was at *peace* until someone or something challenged me, calling me out to battle. Though Peace **does** exist somewhere deep inside of me, it is as if it is lost to me. I have shut the door, choosing to live my life closed off from it. The door *is* my desire to war; my desire to hold onto grudges, arguments, resentments, and my need to be right—this door represents my desire for conflict.

My fear tells me that the door is necessary, that it protects me from intruders. I am afraid that somehow opening the door will kill me. In my mind, Peace has become the enemy; it makes me vulnerable by taking away all my need for defenses. Therefore, the door to my heart remains closed to Peace. Yet, Peace remains, patiently, waiting on the other side of the door, gently, endlessly calling to me. On some level I sense that Peace offers to the warrior inside of me, every solution that I ever hoped to gain with combat, but without the pain and suffering war creates.

Peace continues to call to me; I hear it now over the noise and chaos, the knocking at the door of my heart. The warrior inside of me trembles in fear. I decide not to open the door. Instead, I am content to lean down and peer through the key hole. The trembling subsides; the warrior in me is safe for now.

Objectified;
The Drive-Thru Window of Life

The sign read, "Driver's Entrance," I open the door and enter the small dingy room. Though this is my first delivery for this particular customer, I feel I have been here a hundred times before. It all seems so familiar. The air reeks from a musty pungent odor of sweat and diesel fumes. There are two vending machines, a restroom, and a payphone hanging on the wall. Directly in front of me, there is a counter with a large window, and on it is taped a sign, "Drivers do not open window. Someone will be with you in a moment." Standing directly in front of the window is a frustrated driver, waiting for someone to notice him. Yes, it all seems too familiar; I could shut my eyes and describe the scene completely by memory.

I shut the door behind me and I stand behind the driver at the window to wait my turn. The driver glances at me over his shoulder, "I hope you're ready to take your eight hour break, because you're going to be here a while."

"They're really busy, huh?" I ask.

"No, they're just pissing around, because they know they can. They don't care about us—the drivers. What is it to them how long we wait? They don't pay us for waiting, and later when they're at home asleep in their beds, it isn't them that is still working, driving through the night," he says bitterly.

"How long have you been here?"

"Nearly 4 hours and they haven't even begun to unload me. I was to pickup my next load an hour ago. There is no way I can deliver it on-time and take my break," he says shaking his head back in forth in disgust.

"What are you going to do?"

"The only thing I can do, I guess. I'll drive until I'm too tired to drive anymore, and then I'll pull over and sleep for an hour or two and then I'll keep moving. I hate driving like that, because if I have an accident it will be my neck, but if I don't get it there on-time, everyone will forget that this customer delayed me and it will be my fault it's late."

I nod my head, a gesture that I understand his dilemma, but I say nothing.

Finally, a woman comes to the window, "Look,

driver, as I told you before, you need to wait inside your truck and someone will call you on your CB when they're ready for you. It is as simple as that," she snaps as she slides the window shut again.

The driver groans and begins to mutter profanity as he turns away from the counter. "Good luck," he says to me as he passes. I step forward and stand patiently in front of the window.

After ten minutes pass, I am shocked that no one has acknowledged me. Those inside the office appear oblivious to the fact that I stand just inches away from them. It is as if this huge glass window between us has hidden me from their view. After nearly fifteen minutes I knock lightly on the window. A woman glances up from her desk in my direction, making eye contact with me. I smile. She frowns and quickly looks back down at her paperwork and continues where she left off.

I fold my arms across my chest and begin to breathe deeply as I continue to watch the clock on the wall tick away the minutes. Another ten minutes passes before she rises from her desk and walks toward the counter. As she slides the window slightly open, I am relieved.

"Hello," I say, attempting to forget that she has ignored me for the past thirty-five minutes.

She does not respond to me. While looking down at the paper on the counter in front of her, she asks in a firm voice, "Driver name?"

"My name is joyce cascio."

She continues with a litany of questions, hurling them at me while never looking up: "Company name? Tractor number? Trailer number?"

While I am in mid-sentence answering her questions the phone rings and she raises her left hand in a forcible stopping gesture toward me, as if she is directing traffic. She answers the telephone with her other hand. I stop speaking and wait.

While she is on the telephone, another woman approaches her to sign a pile of forms. After she signs the forms and finishes with her phone call, she hangs up the phone and continues writing notes, ignoring me yet again.

As I stand there, I continue to watch the frenzy of activity before me. There is the ceaseless ringing of telephones; people are moving around from one end of the office to the other; noise from the fork lifts and various other machinery filters into the room each time someone enters or exits the office from the adjacent door which leads to the plant operations.

Finally, the woman returns to the window and continues with her questions in her same firm monotone voice, as if she had never left. I give her the information she requests, but I sense the resentment I am feeling toward her by the tightening I can feel in my chest. She hands me back my paperwork, and directs me to where I am to take my loaded trailer.

Recalling the experience of the earlier driver before me, I decide to inquire about my waiting time, "Do you know how long the wait might be before they begin to unload my trailer?"

"We'll get to you when we get to you," she says as she slides the window shut and walks away.

"Wow, she was probably voted Ms. Congeniality of her class," I think to myself as I walk away. There is nothing left for me to do but to follow her instructions. I think about calling dispatch and telling them I refuse to deliver this load because of this woman's rudeness. Yet, I fear the repercussion from this will be more severe than the treatment I have received here. I would have to drop the load somewhere for another driver to pickup, I would have no way of knowing how far or to where I would have to drive, because I couldn't just drop a loaded trailer anywhere. Also, I could be assigned something really horrid just to teach me not to react in this manner again. Plus, refusing to deliver the load would result in not getting paid for the past two days that I drove to get this load here. No, I wouldn't be spiteful and create more havoc in my life. I keep my frustration to myself, but it doesn't soften the outrage brewing inside of me.

As I walk out to my truck, I feel wounded by the treatment I and the driver before me received, but I am not shocked by it. No, unfortunately, this is not unusual treatment. I often feel that to those on the other side of the counter, including my employer, that I am reduced to nothing more than an extension of my truck—a sub human—a machine.

Climbing into my truck, I shut the door hard. I am beyond angry; I am infuriated. I call Amanda, but she is in a meeting. I toss my cell phone on the passenger seat beside me and I sit staring out the window and begin the waiting game.

While I am waiting there, I recall the many

times since I have been driving this truck that I have been grunted, cursed, and yelled at by dock workers, security guards, and office personnel. This train of thought only fuels my inward hostility further. I think how many times I have pushed myself driving through the night, serious road hazards, snow or rain storms, and heavy traffic or construction, to deliver a load that I may have pulled for five, six, seven hundred miles or more. "All of this for what?" I ask myself. "So, I can be disregarded and treated with disdain by others who believe they are better than me? They assume I am not important, or that I am unintelligent because I drive a truck for a living?"

After two hours passed, I am finally instructed to back my trailer into the dock. I am still agitated, because I am still thinking about how the woman at the counter treated me. "What am I really upset about?" I wonder. I know I was treated rudely, but holding onto to it for hours seems out of proportion with the situation. "If I am going to get this upset every time someone is mean spirited toward me, then this job is going to kill me, because they're all mean," I think. I do not want this job to kill me. I do not want to emotionally shrivel up. Instead, I wanted peace, and I know what I have to do to get it: I need to perceive this situation differently. Otherwise, I will remain trapped by my own circular thinking as I have been for hours. I am ready to move beyond this situation and to find resolution within myself.

I decide to think over the events that I had

experienced again, but this time with a different emphasis. Instead of making myself the center of my focus, I turn my attention to the woman I had issue with. I extend my thoughts to include those inside the office that had completely ignored me. I do not stop there; I include all the offices across the country where I have been treated with disregard. As I close my eyes, I vividly, conjure up in my mind, their faces and hear their words to me, and I can feel myself wanting to get angry again. This time I say, "No," and for the first time, I think about each one of them, standing there in their own circumstances in their offices. I am amazed by the compassion that begins to well up inside of me as I realize how intense the noise and confusion is that engulfs their lives.

I shake my head in disbelief, and almost have to laugh at myself at how ridiculous my previous perceptions had been. These people have no concept of what I have been through to bring them their delivery. They have no idea what it is like to be swallowed up, trapped inside the solitary *belly of the big truck* for hours, days, and weeks on end. No, for them all that exists in their worlds are their offices and what happens inside the walls that surrounds them—"swallows them." They spend their days in a noisy office with people coming and going, hassles, late loads, irate drivers, sick and late employees, upset customers, endless ringing telephones, faxes, computer glare, and office politics.

The ill treatment I thought I had been receiving was not really directed at me personally. I was nothing more than a passing face; I was one of possibly ten, twenty, or more drivers that many of them would see on any given day. Their interactions with me would be no more than a click of a camera lens, and with the flash I would be gone—forgotten. They had too many other things to think about, too many other tasks they were responsible for doing to be concerned about creating a meaningful conversation with me.

No, our conversations would need to be limited to "Driver name," and other basic load specifications, finally ending with, "Driver, please, wait over there." Though I told them my name, they are unable to recall it. "Driver," is easier to remember. It helps them with keeping order to their chaotic day. It keeps me impersonal. To look at the name I had written or to remember it would require too much effort, and multitasking is absorbing every ounce of their energy. Honestly, any further tasks required of them would be an absolute circuit overload.

As I consider these things, I am not so sure I don't prefer the quiet comforts of my big truck. I even find myself feeling pity for them, because I understand their hostility was only a reflection of experiencing the confines of their own *whale*.

"They are as swallowed up as I am," I think to myself. This is an astonishing revelation for me; I would have thought the lesson would end there, but it continued. Thinking about how they reacted to their own confinement made me think about how I treat others from my own *swallowed up* existence.

Before I became a "driver," it never occurred to

me how merchandise was transported. Truck drivers were those annoying individuals who drove recklessly too close to others, and always seemed to be in too big of a hurry. It was as if I lived in a magical world where everything just miraculously appeared in endless supply, as if products grew right from the shelves. Of course that is absurd, but so was my callous disregard for how those products found their way onto those shelves.

Today I observe life differently, because I know every item found anywhere in any store has a history and people are a part of that history. It isn't a simple process; often, there are hundreds of people involved from those who create the products in factories and plants, to those who transport them, unload them, and stock them on the shelves. All of this occurs long before I face those who ring up my items at the check-out counter.

I am shocked by my own blatant disrespect for others. In this moment, I understand that in the eyes of those who I thought had treated me so badly, that actually I have been looking into a mirror of my own reflection. "I am no different from those who treated me with disdain and reduced me to nothing more than an extension of my truck—an object," I say to myself, sadly.

I admit to myself that when I enter a business establishment, I do not see individuals. Instead, I see positions—titles typed on name tags and office desks. For example, I see waitresses or waiters, cashiers, clerks, stockpersons, cooks, chefs, tellers, managers, bankers, directors, teachers, educators, students, doctors, lawyers, etc.

I am disturbed by this revelation, because I know that just as I had been treated, I was also relating to a person's title, thus reducing them to a *role* or *function*. The plain truth is that I lacked empathy and concern for others. When in the check-out line at a store, I was rarely concerned with the name of the cashier. I didn't see this individual as a person. Often times I was too busy watching the prices ring-up to even make eye contact with the individual. I wasn't wondering, "Are you a single parent? Are you responsible for the care of an elderly parent? Are you a college student working your way through school? How are you feeling today? Is life going well for you? Is this where you want to be today? Do you have a life outside of this place?"

No, I was thinking, "Hurry up! I only have a few moments. Can't you go faster? What do you mean you don't carry that item in stock? How much longer? It is all about Me, Me, Me. . . ." No, I did not have to be concerned about the nameless, faceless others in the course of my everyday life—they meant nothing to me.

Certainly, I wished no harm to these nameless individuals, but I did wish them to be quick with ringing up my items, or processing my account information, or getting out of my way in traffic. I wished them not to be a disturbance or disruption in my life. I had grown accustomed to my "drive-thru" convenient lifestyle. "But at what cost do I live this instant gratification that I call life?" I ask myself.

I realize in this moment that life for me has been

diminished to *roles* and *functions*, and a failure to fulfill those *roles* or *functions*, results in a lack of value or usefulness. Just as shippers or customers see me only as a "truck driver," I see them as a *load* accomplished, a means to put money in my pocket. For me, it has become a sterile and uncomplicated way to experience my life.

I wonder, "What must this mean to the titles given to family and friends? Like the titles of partner, wife, sons, mother, sister, brother, father, and friend?"

"This is the *source of all pain*," I hear my heart whisper to me.

"Is this possible, that it is the **source of all pain**?" I ask myself doubtingly.

Before I even finish asking the question, I know it is true; I can feel it. All my pain with others has to do with my relating to *roles* or *functions* they are to fill, and those I am to fill. I rarely interact with others eye to eye, heart to heart.

"How disconnected I have lived these forty some years. How shallow my existence has been," I think to myself. Others exist in my life solely to fill a void, a need. I reduce others as a *means to an end*.

Humbly, I admit to myself that my relationships exist solely for the purpose I deem; likewise, I exist for others solely for the purpose they deem. If the person does not fulfill their purpose, then the relationship becomes worthless, void of meaning. This means I have been having relationships with my own preconceived ideas. People have become merely objects to me; as objects they are either *road blocks* to what I want, or they are believed to be the *fulfillment* to my desires. Either way, I was not experiencing them—but a product.

I have been so busy achieving, reaching for my own fulfillment and my own desires, that I have been completely unaware that I am experiencing life as if it were a "drive-thru window." I have been traveling on the express lane; somewhere along the way I decided that experiencing meaningful interactions with others was too time consuming, too exhausting, and would surely leave me with circuit overload. After all, I am in a hurry! All the billboards and road signs along the way seem to suggest I need to hurry. "But why?" I wonder. "To where do I hurry to go?"

"Away from Intimacy," I hear the same voice within my heart speaking to me.

"Yes, this must be true," I think to myself. Relating to others as a *means to an end* is to use them—to objectify them. Very rarely have there been moments when others truly existed, purely just because they *are*. Rarely have I related to others as the essence of who they are, without an expectation, a goal in mind, a *role* or *function* one of us was to accomplish.

I know that this kind of thinking originated from a belief I secretly held that it would be impossible to love everyone. "Who can love everyone? Who can relate to everyone as if they truly mattered? Who has that kind of time?" I ask. "It isn't possible," is the response I had unconsciously given myself throughout my life.

However, today is different. I am being forced to open my eyes to the muddle and confusion I have been calling my life, so I can truly live, so I can honestly love another purely and unconditionally, and so I can experience intimacy.

I know changing this blueprint will take conscious effort on my part, and that it will not come naturally, as I will be facing a lifetime of beliefs and pre-set patterns. I do not know what such a life will look like or how to approach it exactly. All I know is that embracing this revelation will change the relationships in my life. What I didn't know was how much. . . .

Letting Go

It is the month of May. I am in a field of tall grass. I can feel the wind on my face. A young boy approaches me and in his hands he holds a small raccoon. The sight of the raccoon makes me joyful and a smile spreads across my face; I can barely contain my excitement. I reach out; I want to pet, it to hold it. I can't explain what it is about the little raccoon that has so captured my heart, but I instantly love it. "Can I have him?" I ask.

The little boy looks up at me and with a serious look, "Yes, but you have to promise when he gets big that you will let him go so he can return to the wild to be free."

I agree, reaching out my arms, I eagerly take hold of the little raccoon. "Love never makes prisoners, and nor will I," I think to myself. Yet, the words of the little boy disturb me. Why did he say those words to me? Of course, I do not want to confine the baby raccoon. I know one day he will want to be free, instead of confined in my world. Certainly, it is my hope that he will not stray too far away when I set him free. I would love to watch him grow and have a family of his own one day. For now, I am content to just hold him in my arms.

"Remember your promise," the little boy reminds to me.

"I will," I say, and that was the last thing I remembered before I was startled by a loud sound. I rolled over in the bunk of my big truck. It was 5:00 a.m. I stretched my arm out from my sleeping bag and turned off the alarm clock.

I laid there silently blinking my eyes, straining to see. I was still sleepy. It had all been a dream— the seemingly very real interaction I had with the little boy and the raccoon had never happened. I pulled my sleeping bag up around my shoulders and smiled when I thought about the little boy and his raccoon. But, my smile quickly faded and tears began to sting my eyes, as I realized the dream was about letting go of my sons, especially my youngest son, Seth.

I threw off my sleeping bag and jumped to my feet. I had a convenient pickup appointment which would serve as my distraction, taking my mind off my sons. However, I should have known better. One thing I have learned driving a big truck, is that it is the last place a person should go to escape his or her thoughts. So many hours of isolation only brings one's avoided thoughts nearer. As each day passed, my solitude brought me many insights as I edged closer and closer to understanding and accepting the truth about the many adversities in my life.

One realization I had come to recently was that finances had not been the only reason I accepted this job. Though I had not wanted to admit it, being away from home had appeared enticing because of the ever growing tension that existed between my two sons and I. It was not that I did not want to be home, but that I felt I had lost all objectivity and that I no longer knew how to be home in a way that was respectful and peaceful for everyone involved.

It was a strange dichotomy, my relationship with them. Inside my heart lived a million still images that I had captured over the years. It was my own photo album of memories: holidays, birthdays, school plays, teacher conferences, band concerts, family vacations, family meetings, first girlfriends, driving lessons, jobs, proms, and on and on. Recalling these memories brought me both smiles and happy tears. On the road, I was tortured by the distance that seemed to separate us. Whenever I returned home, I found the same old weary battle lines that we had previously drawn, as we were still waging the same war. It was discouraging to discover the distance between us was far greater than the miles that had seemed to separate us.

I could never understand why our relationships were so full of conflict when my intensions were to convey the love I felt for both of them. Yet, Amanda and the boys often accused me of having unrealistic expectations of our family life. Their most common statement to me was, "We're not the Brady Bunch," because that was what they thought I was trying to create. There is an old saying, "The road to hell is paved with good intentions." I did not know it at the time, but my so called "loving" intentions were creating a living hell for my family and me. By the time my boys' senior year of high school had arrived, our relationships had diminished to arguing, yelling, and slamming doors, as outward signs of our having shut one another out. My climbing into the big truck six months ago had been my attempt to run away, to escape. In the end, I had to admit that it had changed nothing.

As I drove the open road before me, my mind drifted back and forth between my two sons. I thought of Matthew, my elder son by nine weeks. Though he is Amanda's biological son, I had known him since he was seventeen months old. When he turned eight years old, I became his step-mom, and I loved him as though he were my own natural born child.

Matt has so many wonderful talents and gifts to offer the world. He is a deep thinker, intelligent, hardworking, and handsome. He can also be stubborn, determined, and a rebel without a cause, including at home. Amanda and I had few rules, but Matt seemed determined to challenge them all, as

Letting Go

each week brought him not only closer to graduation but to his 18th birthday. Conflicts with Matt, though frustrating, were usually quiet; when he was angry, he kept to himself; punishing Amanda and I with his silence.

I wanted to cry as I thought about how difficult and strained our time together had become. My last trip home had been an eventful one. Matt had asked if a friend could stay over, and though Amanda had to work the next day, we had agreed, providing they kept the noise down. At 5:00 a.m. the next morning, I woke up and went downstairs to find the front door slightly open. This made me suspicious, and I went to investigate. When I did not find either son or their friend in the house, I went out into the yard and barn to look for them. I did not find them anywhere, but in the barn I found evidence that a party had taken place. This was further, confirmed when I saw the vomit on the steps leading into the house. Around 6:00 a.m. a car pulled into our driveway and our sons and their friends staggered out and went up to the front door. It was evident that Matt was still drunk, as he swayed back and forth, barely able to climb the front steps. I met them there, and it would be an understatement to say that "we had words" that day. We exchanged many words, fierce and hurtful ones. When all was said and done, we all agreed that Matt would move out after graduation.

The truth was that I did not want Matt to move out. I wanted him to stay with us, but I wanted him to be different. It was difficult not to take his actions as a rejection, instead of a teenager coming of age, growing up. He wanted to define himself, but he could not do it while he lived in our shadows. He needed to be free to make his own rules to live by and to become the man he desired to be. To do this, he needed our support, but not in the way I wanted to give it. Amanda and I agreed to pay his deposit and first's month rent on his apartment after graduation. I was still reeling from that decision.

I glance at the digital clock on the dashboard. It is 9:00 a.m., and I wonder if Seth is awake yet. Seth is our youngest son, and I fell in love with him the moment the nurse placed him in my arms 17 years earlier. He is witty, fun loving, free in his expressions, handsome and intelligent. He is also assertive and can be demanding. When Seth thinks he is right about an issue, he becomes extremely vocal and confrontational, fighting to the bitter end. Watching him mature over the years has been like looking into a mirror. Sometimes, looking into this mirror has been difficult for me; we share many similar traits.

My conflicts with Matt were confined to when I was at home. Sadly, even on the road, my conflicts with Seth continued. The marvels of modern technology made it possible for our feuds to survive via my cell phone.

Though Seth and I had many conflicts, depending on the flavor of the day, there was one issue that had plagued our relationship for years— his school attendance. Similar to many teenagers, Seth hated school. To him, school had only one benefit, and it was purely social. Making things even more challenging was the fact that Seth was not a morning person and he often overslept. For this reason, mornings in the Cascio household were often turbulent.

Since Amanda's schedule required her to be at work before me, the task for waking Seth and ensuring that he made it to school became my responsibility. Yet, even I had to leave for work before his classes started, and there were many times he decided to go back to bed after I had left the house. For years, my life had been filled with weekly calls from his school's attendance office informing me that Seth was either tardy or absent.

I had thought this trend would improve once Seth became a senior, but it did not. By the time I had begun to drive my big truck, Seth was the tardiest and most absent person in his class. I tried to remedy this situation with daily phone calls once I arrived at work, to ensure that he was still awake and on his way to school. When I began driving my big truck, I had continued this daily ritual. However, these calls seldom went well.

Though our three or four minute conversations began innocently enough, they would soon erupt into verbal confrontation. The calls had a repetitive quality to them. I usually began with a cheery, "Good Morning, my young son." I usually received the greeting of a grumpy teenager, "What do you want, mom?"

Our usual script went something like this: "Seth, do you know what time it is?" or "Seth what time do you plan to be at school today?"

"Mom, I thought you were not going to call me anymore in the mornings!"

"I know, I just was thinking of you and I wanted to call," I lied. I knew well this was a premeditated phone call.

However, Seth never bought the lie; "Bull Shit," was usually his reply.

That is when I would switch into lecture mode, "Seth, you know, you can't miss any more school. You are not going to graduate if you continue to miss classes. What about the make-up tests you've missed and your late homework assignments? Really, Seth, what are you thinking?"

Seth would interrupt, "What the Hell! I thought you were going to let me be responsible for myself. I've got it all under control and you don't have to worry about it! I am almost eighteen years old! Let me live my life! Jesus Christ!!"

Usually by the time he finished these words, I was holding the phone several inches away from my ear to avoid hearing impairment. "Seth, you don't have it under control, which is why I am calling you. You were still asleep and you have to be at school in less than an hour. If I hadn't called, you would have overslept!"

"Stop yelling at me! I don't have to be at school today until 10:30 a.m."

"**Seth**, I am **not yelling** at you! **You are yelling at me! I am just responding to you!** Come on, Seth, what a bunch of B.S. that you don't have to be at school until later. I just talked to the school and they don't have any idea where you are. **Now, get up and get to school!**" I would demand in as threatening a tone as possible.

"**You don't know! You aren't here! Stop bothering me!**"

So there we were, our battle lines clearly defined, drawn across the airwaves with both of us talking over the other, interrupting. Usually, our calls ended by one of us hanging up on the other, and with a personal vow to myself that I would not call him again. I would try to reason within myself that if he did not graduate, he could attend school next year to make up the missed credits, or that he could take his G.E.D. By the next morning, a subtle form of amnesia would come over me, and I would find myself repeating the events from the day before, as if I thought the outcome might be different—it never was. I knew we were caught in a bad script, but that did not prevent me from using it.

When the first week of May arrived I decided to change tactics. I called my mother who lived in Tucson to enlist her help by making her my partner in coercion. I told her the severity of the situation, and asked her to call Seth daily to wake him up. She agreed. Instead of calling Seth each morning, I began to call my mother to remind her that she needed to call Seth. I thought I had cleverly handled this situation—that I had finally won. I secretly reveled in my self-perceived victory.

However, when the objective becomes that of *winning* and *losing* in a relationship, it is never smooth, it is never easy, and the results do not last.

In short, it never works. I should not have popped the cork on my victory bottle of organic apple cider so quickly. Regrettably, my scheme only worked for one week. The following week, Amanda called me to report that the school had called and that Seth had missed three days of school that week. "What had happened?" I wondered. My plans seemed perfect but evidently, not perfect enough.

When I called my mother to inquire, I learned that she had not repetitively called Seth, as I had done. When he did not answer the phone, she assumed he had already left for school and she went on with her day. I could not believe he was doing this. I felt outraged. Graduation was so close and we had family coming into town for the celebration. On cue, I began playing my part in our familiar script. I called and called and called each morning until Seth answered the phone.

Administering punishment had never been a strong area for me. I never believed it was effective in accomplishing long term results; at best it only provided short term success. However, I had forgotten all of that as graduation approached and I was desperate. With only three weeks remaining before graduation, I only needed short term results. I began to threaten Seth with loss of privileges if he did not go to school, and the struggle between us continued though I was hundreds, even thousands of miles away.

"Ah, a reprieve from my thoughts," I said to myself as I arrived at my customer's location in Muscatine, Iowa. It was 9:30 a.m. as I drove onto

Letting Go

the lot of the dog food processing plant. I was immediately overwhelmed by the putrid smell that emitted from the factory, and nearly gagged. Once I parked my truck, I quickly went inside the office building. A short round middle aged woman came to the window. I gave her my load number. "Another Paradise driver just left a few minutes ago with that load," she said.

"Wow, really? Do you have another load for Paradise?" I asked, thinking possibly I had been given the wrong load number.

"No, that was it. No other loads going out with Paradise today. Maybe you should call your dispatcher to figure out what happened."

I called my dispatcher, and she was as confused as I was. She instructed me to wait there until she figured out what had happened or until I could be assigned another load. I knew the timing could not be worse, because it was Friday and it was my weekend to go home. Usually, loads allowing a driver to go home were picked days ahead. Now they would have to scramble to find me another less planned load that somehow someway might get me home. The thought of having to spend any additional time on the road was overwhelming. I had been gone for more than two weeks, and at that moment, only four hours separated me from home. With this mix-up I had no idea what would happen. As I exited the building to go outside and wait inside of my big truck, I hoped for the best but dreaded the worst.

I looked at my watch. It was 10:00 a.m. I

wondered if Seth had made it to school. I knew he was up late working on a project that he was supposed to present in one of his classes today. I decided to call him. I did not know it then, but this situation was about to hit crescendo proportions resulting in a life altering experience for us both.

When he did not answer, I thought possibly he had gone to work at the guidance office, because he was scheduled to work there daily from 9:30 to 11:00 a.m. filing papers and running various errands to earn a work study credit. He was often late or absent from this class, especially on Fridays. I called the secretary, Gail, but she was not in her office. Her temporary assistant who answered the phone explained that she had not seen Seth all morning.

I was furious! I was certain he was at home sleeping. I continued to call, but he did not answer. I called and called and called, and by 11:00 a.m., in a panic, I began to leave messages filled with threats. "Seth, if you are there you had better get up and get to school, because I am on my way home. I am less than 4 hours away, and trust me I will have this big truck in overdrive. **Do you hear me**? I am on my way home, and when I get there, if you are there, I am going to kick your ass for every time I did not do it in the past! I have had it! **This is the final straw!**" I yelled into the phone.

I waited a few moments and then called again. I called again and again until it was 12:00 noon. By this time, I had begun to give in. All hope seemed lost that Seth would ever graduate. Still, I left another threatening message. "Seth, if you do not go to school today you better have your clothes packed by the time I arrive home. I am taking you to the Salvation Army to live, because that is where you are headed if you do not graduate. You will be homeless, so let's just skip all the in between steps and go straight to homelessness! I mean it, Seth! If you've never believed anything I have said, you better believe this! If you are not at school today, you will be out of there tonight!"

I was sobbing. I called my mother and told her the situation, and between the two of us, we left Seth over eleven messages. My mother's messages were much more colorful and threatening then mine. She might be sixty some years old, but she is as spunky and tough as anyone I have ever known.

By 1:00 p.m.; I had been sitting there for three hours. My frustration was growing. It was growing with Seth, and it was growing with Paradise. Finally, Paradise's Customer Service Department realized what I had known for hours, that they had made a mistake and that there was no load for me at this customer. I would be re-assigned a load, but I would have to wait until the details were worked out. I did not want to wait. I wanted to go home. My family needed me. Seth needed me. I wanted out of this truck. I hated trucking! I laid my face in my hands and cried.

Waiting there, my entire life felt like it was out of control. I felt powerless. I was too far away to get to Seth, and I could not change anything about my load assignment. "I could just get out of my truck and walk away," I thought. This was a fantasy I envisioned every day at least once, but my truck was full of my personal belongings, and realistically I could not carry them all with me. To make matters worse, Amanda was attending an off-site conference, and it would be hours before I could reach her by phone or before she would be available to pick me up. I did not want to be stranded someplace waiting for a ride for more hours than it would take for me to leave here on my own. Plus, there was that little detail of the $3,700.00 I would owe for my training if I walked away now. I knew walking away would only complicate and inflame the situation more, so I stayed.

I sat there in my truck, feeling stranded and trapped. The smell from the factory was almost more than I could bear. I had resorted to breathing through my mouth to control my urge to vomit. Finally, I received my new load assignment. I would have to go west to Cedar Rapids, Iowa, the opposite direction from my home in Rockton, Illinois. There, I would pickup a load with a delivery appointment for tomorrow near Chicago. This meant I would not return home until sometime late tomorrow afternoon. I was disappointed. I sobbed uncontrollably. I kept asking myself, "Why is this happening?"

My mind was racing with a million thoughts. I felt completely overwhelmed. I decided to call Seth again. At the beep, instead of yelling, I remained calm but began with my usual lecture, "Seth, you need to show up for life! No one else can do that for you! No one can show up for your life but you! You can't always take the easy way out!" I was still speaking when the answering machine beeped and abruptly cut me off.

With those words still echoing in my thoughts, I laid my hands and head over the steering wheel and cried what felt like a river of tears. The pain I was feeling was agonizing. After several minutes, I raised my head and looked out across the concrete lot to the raggedy warehouse in front of me. And for the first time, I wondered who it was I was really talking to when I had said those words. Was I talking to Seth or was I talking to myself? I didn't know anymore.

I thought about my life sitting there in that parking lot, surrounded by dilapidated buildings and that horrific smell. I believed I had been everything but successful in my life. I was less than 7 weeks away from my 41st birthday, and I felt as if my entire life were a tragic train wreck—that I had failed at everything I had ever tried to accomplish, including motherhood. In that moment, I realized my reactions and urgency toward Seth had little to do with him and much more to do with me. I knew Seth was a mirror for me, and that I had been projecting onto him a lot of what I believed to be my own inadequacies. I had been too stubborn to listen to my own Spirit and I had wanted to spare him from experiencing the same pain. I was living vicariously through Seth, trying to save myself. I hated to think that this is how I had been living and reacting with him. "No wonder he had to be so obstinate and rebellious. It was his defense against me—it was how he had survived," I said, marveling at my own ignorance. "Seth has spent his entire life fighting me for the control of his life," I thought.

After all of these months, even years of struggling with Seth, I decided to ask God for help. It was not as if I had not prayed before about our relationship—I had, possibly hundreds even thousands of times, but this time I prayed differently. I prayed with an honest heart, "God, I am *powerless* over Seth. . . . I have no control over him or the decisions he makes. . . . Ultimately it is Seth who will decide his fate—not me. . . . I have spent the past seventeen years trying to control the outcome of his life. I have tried to enforce penalties and manipulate situations to get particular results, only to realize I can't guarantee the outcome. Please, God, help me to find peace in this situation, because I am tormented by it. I am ready to *accept* that it is impossible to control another, that I am powerless to control Seth or anyone else. The only person I can ever have power over is me."

There it was; the true core of what all of our arguing was about—my control issues. I wanted the power in Seth's and Matt's lives because I believed I knew what was *right* for both of them. I was so caught up in my need to be *right*—to argue my point—to make them understand me that I was missing the relationship I could have with them. Sadly, I had to admit to myself that though Matt and Seth were my sons, I had been treating them no differently than the nameless others I had objectified

Letting Go

throughout my life.

"How can this be," I wondered, "that I could objectify even the closest of my relationships?" It was bad enough to do this with a nameless "stranger," a clerk at a store, but it was something entirely different to do it with my children.

"Was it? Was it really that different?" I questioned myself.

I knew my core beliefs transcended all areas of my life. Beliefs are not compartmentalized, reserved for one area and not another. My core beliefs are present in all areas of my life, even though I may attempt to express it differently or to camouflage it. This is exactly what I had been doing with my issue of *objectifying* and *control*. My relationship with my sons had been so focused on the "mother/son" definition of what *should be* that I had failed to see them as individuals or to see their needs. To me they existed only as *sons*. That was their role to play. Mine was to play the part of *mother*. My sons were fighting me for their own survival, fighting me for their right to exist—apart and separate from me or my preconceived roles.

These thoughts frightened me. I wanted to resist them. They called into question, not only the very feelings I had been justifying my entire life as *love*, but my understandings about being a mother. It should be no surprise, I argued fiercely, defending my position and my past behavior. "What would happen to Seth if I was not there to take care of him? He obviously needed me or I would not have to call him. He was the one oversleeping, not me. He was the one who needed to graduate, not me." In the end, I concluded he was the responsible one. It was he who was bringing all this upon himself.

"Phooey," I thought to myself, "No one can live without these rules or these roles society has given to us, so why should I try? As a parent, it is my right, my duty!" I said, as I rallied myself to call home again, rejecting the insight that was attempting to penetrate my resistance. When I called, Seth still did not answer the phone. I thought this was odd because I knew even Seth would be awake by this time of day. Then it occurred to me that I should call his school's Attendance Office. They would have a record of Seth's attendance.

When I called Hononegah High School and spoke with the Attendance Office secretary, I was told that Seth was at school and that he had been there all day. I felt a mixture of relief and regret. I was relieved he was at school, but I had left so many messages and I had no way to erase them. I knew he would be the first one home and he would hear them—all of them. I sat there stunned and bewildered. Emotionally, I felt as if I had just hit a brick wall.

"How could I possibly consider any of what I said on those messages as love? How could I stand behind those words and support them in anyway?" I tearfully asked myself. I knew I could not.

Sitting there, quietly self reflecting, I decided to let go. It did not matter that dealing with this issue was painful for me; it had become too painful not to deal with it. I was sickened and amazed by all the time I had wasted pursuing control in my relationships. "What is behind this beast, this control, which drives me onward, lurking even in the darkest hidden corners of my life?" I thought. "What is it that makes me frantically reach-out, grasping wildly, clingingly, imposing my will on that of others?" I asked.

"Lack of trust," I felt these words inwardly.

"But, I do trust. I am trusting," I argued with myself.

"How deep is that trust?" was the question.

"Clearly, not deep enough," I had to answer. I knew, in many cases, the trust I felt was only surface deep. I did not trust situations or events in my life to turn out the way I had wanted or envisioned, and that is why I fought so hard to control them. Though I tried, I could not remember one argument that I ever had with either son that had changed them. I had to concede that controlling another individual was really an illusion. In all my attempts to control, I had been unsuccessful.

I had to accept that what I had been calling love was not love, but a list of demands or ultimatums. Finally, for the first time, it was crystal clear to me; all those areas of my life where I felt most compelled to control were the areas I had the *least trust*.

At that moment I thought, "To **accept** the things I have no control over is the most responsible and peaceful choice I can make; to do otherwise, is a misuse of my own personal power." My dilemma was to determine where my personal power ended and another's begun.

In a last feeble attempt, I asked, "As a parent, am I not to *defend, protect,* and *serve* where my children seem unable to do so for themselves? If so, then what form should my defense take?"

"All forms and acts of defense are primitive, a call to war. Therefore, to engage in defense is a violent way to live," my soul provided. My relationship problems had nothing to do with changing others. Instead, it was personal—it was me. My healing lay not in my deep involvement with others, but in my focusing on my personal lack of trust.

That night as I crawled into my bunk to go to sleep, I was sad but relieved. I knew that letting go would be a process, and that today I had begun that process. My eyes were opened by this experience. From now on, there was no place control could hide undetected in my life, even when it was cleverly disguised as "helping" others as I had tried to convince myself I was doing with Seth. After that day, I never called Seth again to wake him up for school, and that is when I learned for certain what he had always known—he never needed me to. Seth never missed another day of school.

Three weeks later, Matt and Seth walked across the graduation stage and received their diplomas while Amanda and I cheered, along with several aunts, cousins, their uncle, and grandmother (my mother) who all had flown in to witness and share this joyous event in their lives. It was a wonderful weekend filled with healing and love.

As planned on June 1st, Matt moved into his new apartment down the street from us. Then on July 3rd, we took Seth to the airport so he could spend the summer with my mother in Tucson. After the summer, he decided to remain in the desert. He moved into his own apartment in Scottsdale, Arizona. And just like that, both boys had what they wanted most—to become masters of their own fate.

This transition of letting go continues to transform my life. More than ever, I understand that life is what each of us will make of it, and no one is qualified to direct or coerce another into anything. I know that parents are often led to believe that it is they who teach their children to *grow up*. I have come to believe that this is not true. Yes, I raised my children, by housing their bodies, but I did not teach them to *grow up*. Instead, it is they who have taught me to grow up. As a parent I learned to become less selfish; learned there was more to life than my wants or needs, and now I am learning to let go of my need to control. Through my sons, I have learned what it means to live honestly, fully, completely. If someone were to ask me today, "Who has been my greatest teacher?" I would have to answer, "My sons."

There are days when I affectionately remember my dream of the little boy and his raccoon, and I am reminded of a familiar poem, "If you love something, set it free. If it comes back to you, it is yours. If it doesn't, then it never was." Now, the only part of this poem that stands out to me is the first sentence.

"If you love something, set it free." Today, I understand that if I have really done this, then the remaining two sentences are completely void of meaning. Loving another has nothing to do with them accepting or rejecting my love. Love is all that exists, once I have let go of everything else. Love just is. . . . Now it was up to me to sift through the confusion I had called attachments, responsibilities, and love. The challenge was recognizing them for what they really were—my attempts to control others. What I would do with this information remained to be seen.

Time to Forget; Independence Day

It is mid-July; the air is thick and muggy. When I breathe in, the air is hot as it enters my mouth, traveling down my throat and into my lungs. My chest feels heavy as I labor for each breath. My eyes sting from the humid heat. I am drenched in sweat.

I am frustrated; I have called my dispatcher and I have sent messages over my computer system, but to no avail. So, I do what is expected of me: I sit and wait. I have been sitting here for hours. It is a condition that occurs too frequently. It is common to wait two, three, even five hours for a load assignment. Though I think that is an unreasonable amount of time to wait—I have seen worse.

Unfortunately for me and other drivers, it is not unusual to wait ten, fifteen, even twenty hours to be dispatched, loaded, or unloaded at various locations.

Though I know I should be accustomed to such treatment by now, I am not. After nearly seven months, I still allow myself to get upset by the waiting, even when I know it is part of the madness of the trucking industry. It seems unfair, this imbalance of power my company seems to wield over me. For the entire 14-21 days I am away from home, I am never without my truck or the responsibilities associated with it, but the only time I am able to earn money is when driving. All of the time I spend waiting is free, that is unless it exceeds 24 hours, at which time I can receive "lay-over pay" in the amount of $80.00 for the day. I have come to interpret this excessive waiting time as an indicator of my value to my employer, whom I have come to believe does not value me or my time. This has resulted in continuous battles between me and my dispatcher.

As I sit smoldering in the summer's heat I feel hopeless. I entertain thoughts of quitting, but I remind myself that in another 5 ½ months I will have fulfilled my training obligation, and then I can walk away with no penalties. On days like today, I am hot, tired, and discouraged, and it seems there is no light at the end of the tunnel; my self pity takes over, leading me into a downward spiral. This descent into my own private hell always leads me to the same muddled conclusions—that I am a failure, and my life, lacking purpose, has become nothing more than a waste land. I want to raise the white flag and surrender.

Finally, my computer beeps, breaking the silence and the torment of my mind. It is mid-afternoon. As I study the assignment, I take in a deep breath and slowly exhale as I experience a mixture of emotions. I am to pick up an empty trailer in Seville, Ohio where I am sitting, and drive it a whopping 18 miles to a customer's location in Wooster, Ohio. Once I arrive, it is estimated that I will have a 3 hour wait while I am live-loaded. Once my trailer is loaded, I am to drive the 18 miles back to Seville, Ohio and drop this load at our Operating Center for another driver to deliver. I am told the market is "soft" and this is the best they can offer me for today. I am assured that tomorrow I will be given a better load. I quickly do the math. I will work the entire day and I will be paid approximately $35.00 for my labor. Normally, after waiting so many hours to receive a load which has so few miles, I would immediately become furious, calling or messaging my dispatcher.

However, this time is different. I don't call my dispatcher. Instead, I sit motionless, staring at the computer screen. Wooster, Ohio wasn't just any random city to me; it was a city with which I had a past. Instinctively, I knew this load wasn't about money, miles, or my job—it was about opening another closed door within my heart. I take a deep breath and sigh. Turning the ignition key, I start the engine of my big truck. While the air pressure begins to build, I reach for my map to find directions. A few minutes later I drive out of the gate. I am on my way to Wooster, Ohio.

As I drive, my mind becomes filled with fragmented memories of my youth, taking me back to a place and time I had long ago forgotten—to Wooster, Ohio. It was the place of my earliest childhood memories. Though I had lived in Belpre, Ohio, a small town in the Southern part of the state for the first six months of my life, I didn't remember it. At six months of age, my mother married a man from Wooster, and he moved us there.

I had many wonderful experiences in Wooster for most of my nine years there, but there was a mixture of highs and lows. When I was fifteen months old, my sister Theresa was born. However, the marriage between our mother and her father did not last, ending bitterly. When I was four years old, my mother met and married another man from Wooster, and later when I was almost six years old, my brother Charlie was born.

Wooster is where I spent my summers climbing trees, catching lightening bugs, playing with cars and trucks in our driveway, playing with my sister and brother, and digging holes in the family garden. The latter always upset my stepfather who wanted to know, what on earth possessed me to dig holes in his garden? I always responded, "I am digging an underground tunnel, like on the television show Hogan's Hero's." "Tunnels are deeper than two feet," he'd say annoyed, but that never stopped me. Every summer I was out there digging with all my might until I hit rock and then I would give up, moving over a few feet, I'd begin to dig again.

A Time to Forget; Independence Day

It was in Wooster that I received my first bike on my sixth birthday. It was a gift from my grandparents. I can still remember the care my grandfather took as he painted it a deep navy blue with a white stripe down the side. I taught myself to ride that bike going down hill. I enjoyed going downhill because the momentum allowed me to remain upright longer, before I came crashing down, skinning my knees.

It was in Wooster that every spring, I would chase baby rabbits around the three acre yard where we lived. My mother and stepfather had agreed, after much insistence from me, that I could keep one if I could catch it. Of course, I never did! They were too fast, but what delight I experienced diving and tumbling in the summer's grass behind them.

Yes, Wooster was the place of my earliest memories, and where I learned a sense of family. I had managed for the past thirty-two years to rarely mention this place to anyone, even myself. Actually, no one in my family, not my mother or my siblings wanted to discuss Wooster, Ohio, or the years we lived there. Wooster was like a dark black cloud that left a painful imprint on each of us; it was a place and time we all seemed to want to block out, to forget. Yet, none of us really forgot this place or the things that happened there.

My sister can still remember in vivid detail the day my stepfather picked her up by her arm and threw her into a mirror that hung on the bedroom closet door. He was angry because she couldn't find her slip and she was going to be late for kindergarten. She spent the remainder of that day in the emergency room getting stitches sewn into her head. Her head would heal, but all these years later her heart still has not.

My mother recalls numerous beatings she received from my stepfather. Yet, the one she remembers the most is the day he nearly beat her to death. My stepfather, having gotten lost in one of his rages, was beating my sister and me uncontrollably. My mother pleaded with him to stop, but he pushed her away. She searched frantically around the room for something to use in her defense against him. That is when she grabbed the iron from the ironing board and raised it up, threatening him. This is the last thing she remembers before waking up in the hospital with her head and face bruised and swollen beyond recognition.

I remember the screaming, the fighting, the black eyes and busted lips. I remember the nearly daily beatings I received. I remember sitting down to eat a spaghetti dinner that ended up on my head and lap as the bowl was hurled through the air before it thudded against the wall; my mother didn't, in my stepfather's words, "make it right."

I remember the time my mom was pregnant, but her pregnancy was aborted because my stepfather kicked her in the stomach. I remember so many times I hysterically dialed zero, to ask the operator to send the police because my dad was going to kill my mother and us. The police would come and remove my stepfather from our house, but he always returned, usually the same night. I remember the terror, the fear, the hiding, the nightmares, and the agony of never being able to escape.

By the time I was nine years old, my stepfather's temper had become completely unpredictable. I was the oldest of my siblings and I had the most to fear from him, because I was expected to set the example and to take care of them. It was a task that I often fell short in performing, which always ended with a harsh beating from my stepfather. My mother, fearing for my safety, sent me to live with my grandparents in Belpre, Ohio. I was happy with my grandparents in a way that I had never experienced before that time, but even Belpre wasn't far enough away to make the nightmares stop. Consequently, those nightmares would continue to haunt my dreams for the next twenty years.

Though my terror only remained in the form of a nightmare, the literal terror continued for my mother and my siblings whom I had left behind in Wooster, Ohio. However, that same year, while my mother was working as a waitress in a restaurant, she waited on a man who she remembers to this day, though she never knew his name.

"What can I get for you?" she asked.

His response was not what she expected. In a gentle and kind voice he asked her, "Tell me about your reoccurring dream?"

"What?" my mother asked, somewhat taken back by the words of this customer.

"The dream you've been having that is troubling you," he said.

"I haven't told anyone about my dreams," she said shocked. She looked at the man again and she didn't know why but she felt she could trust him. She sat down at his table and quickly told him her dream. "I keep having a dream where I am with my mother and we are driving over the Belpre Bridge and the bridge begins to collapse and as we are falling I am scared because I do not know how to swim and I am afraid I am going to drown."

"Your dream is about change. You will not drown. You will survive; but if you stay in the situation you are in, you will not survive. You must leave him," he said. That is when my mother told the man about her marriage and how she had been planning to leave for years but was afraid her husband would kill her if she did.

"You have more to fear if you stay," he told her. Their entire conversation only lasted a few moments but it was powerful. Later, my mother recognized this same man on the Phil Donahue show. He was a psychic who could hold the telephone cord and would tell callers about their lives. That is when my mother gained the courage she needed to leave. My mother filed for divorce, and a short time later moved to Belpre, Ohio. There we lived with my grandparents for several months until she was able to save enough money to move the four of us into an apartment of our own. As time passed, Wooster became a faint memory to us all.

Now, here I was, thirty-two years later, being given a load assignment requiring me to return to this town. I knew, at this time in my life, this event

A Time to Forget; Independence Day

was no coincidence, but destiny. Still, I wondered, "Why Wooster and why now?" I believed I held no animosity, hatred, or anger toward the man who I had once called, *father*, nor did I believe I had any unfinished business with this town. Yet, little did I know, all of those beliefs were about to change.

As I near Wooster, Ohio, Amanda calls me on my cell phone. I tell her I am on my way to Wooster, Ohio and I remind her that is where I lived until I was nine years old. "Wow, I didn't realize you lived there that long," she says. She agrees that there must be some healing or gift in this trip for me. As we are talking, I see the sign for Wooster, but before I can end our conversation, I pass the exit that I intended to take.

I drive to the next exit, but it does not allow me to loop back onto the highway. In one quick instant, my carefully prepared directions become useless. Suddenly, I am driving in downtown Wooster on narrow roads with no idea where I am. I immediately begin to ask for directions on my CB radio, but a short in my cable causes a weak connection. My heart is pounding. It never seems to fail when I am faced with situations like these that there is no place for me to safely stop or to pull off onto the side of the road. No, I must keep driving or come to a complete stop in the middle of the road, which is impossible to do without severe repercussions. So, I keep driving slowly, cautiously through town. I urgently look for anything familiar, anything from my past that I can rely on for direction. I find myself driving past the college. I experience momentary relief; as a child I remember passing this way hundreds of times. Unfortunately, as an adult, so much seems to have changed that I feel as though this is my first trip here.

I continue driving, but I begin to have difficulty maneuvering my big truck, as each turn seems to lead me onto another smaller, narrower road. I can feel myself becoming anxious. I am worried I might get a ticket for driving in a no truck zone; even worse, I might get stuck with no way to turn my truck around. Though full of static, the signal on my CB, becomes clearer, and finally a driver close enough hears me in my distress. He tells me, "Driver, turn down Beal Street and follow it to the end and turn left on Liberty Street." The driver continues to give me directions, but I stop listening to him.

"Liberty Street!" I think to myself. "Liberty Street! I remember living off Liberty Street, riding my bike on Liberty Street, walking to the store, the ice cream shop, and to school on Liberty Street." As I continue to drive, I search desperately not so much for the customer as I am searching for signs of anything familiar—anything of my past life here. When I reach Liberty Street, there is only a vague recollection of this place I once knew; it appears as unfamiliar as the college had been to me. Finally, when I reach the customer's location, I am told I will need to wait for several hours. Reluctantly, I drive around to the back of the building to wait.

Sitting there looking out at the neighborhood surrounding me, I begin to experience a strange sensation. I think that I recognize some of the older houses; as I look around, this place does seem oddly familiar. I wonder if I have been here before, or if my mind is playing tricks on me. The longer I sit there, the more I sense I am close to the place I once lived. Maybe, I am even sitting in part of the field where I once lived, but there is no way to know for certain.

As the hours pass slowly, I think of nothing else but the nine years I lived in this city. Recalling these memories made it all seem so real, like it was just yesterday; but it hadn't been yesterday or the day before or the year before. It had been thirty-two years ago! "How is this possible, that just being in this place brings it all back to me?" I wonder.

Though I want deeply to believe I am living in the present, I know I am not. It is clear this is not the same Wooster I remember. In my rational mind I knew the Wooster from my childhood did not exist anymore. Regardless of the events I had experienced, life here had moved on. There was not any door I could knock on and the person answering on the other side would know me. No one here knows anything about the skinny frightened girl I had been, or my family. The police officers who had so frequently visited our house during those years had since moved away, retired, or passed on from this life. Having moved away at such a young age, I had no friends here. I didn't even recognize most of the city, because over the years buildings had been torn down and new ones had been erected to stand in their place. "Yes," I admit to myself, "there are new histories being written on these streets, and there are no ghosts that remain here, except the ones in my own head."

I am not experiencing a new phenomenon; it is not mysteriously "coming back to me" because I am here in Wooster. In essence, I have never left Wooster, and Wooster has never left me. What I am experiencing is my own on-going relationship with the past—a past with a city I once knew as Wooster, Ohio. It is a reflection of my tightly held memories that has left my life submerged in fear.

"What could I possibly gain by holding onto memories that are so painful and frightening to me?" I ask myself.

The word "Martyrdom!" enters my mind.

"Martyrdom?" I exclaim, both shocked and insulted by my own thoughts. "How can this be?" I ask firmly?

I understand too well the concept of martyrdom, because I had been teaching others about it for years in workshops and classes. Historically, the term martyr was used to describe "selfless acts of love," even when such acts could lead to one's death, especially relating to dying for one's religious faith. For many, such "selflessness" has been praised as the greatest example or expression of love, thus leading Martyrdom to become one of the greatest false symbols of love that many people unwittingly spend their lives aspiring to, including myself. Typically, playing the martyr means sacrificing one's self for the benefit of others, and then feeling resentment later when others do not respond in the way one had hoped or desired them to act. Martyrdom is a deceitful form of manipulation used to gain power over others while pretending to be "selfless," and most people tend to use it in some way until we make a conscious choice to communicate differently.

Feeling pressure in my chest, I lean my head against my driver side window and attempt to turn my attention to the birds chirping, the wind blowing lightly through the trees, and the sounds of passing cars. Though I want to ignore what I am feeling inside, I can not. An avalanche of haunting memories is bombarding me and I can not run away from them or what they signify—Martyrdom.

"But I forgave my stepfather," I say in my defense. "I don't hold him accountable for what happened all those years ago. In fact, I even pity him because I think him a sad man, incapable of loving. I hold no ill feelings toward him."

I sit silently for an unspecified time, and then I breathe in deeply. As I exhale, tears well up in my eyes, because I can hear the messenger of truth whispering to my heart telling me, "I never forgave my stepfather." Now, I can understand why the mere mention of Wooster causes a flood of memories to come rushing to the surface. At best, I had pardoned or extended a reprieve to him, but never forgiveness.

"Is there really a difference" I wonder silently.

"Yes," my soul answers, "to *forgive* means to relinquish *all* memories that cause me harm and to only remember the memories that unite or bring me closer to others. To *pardon*, on the other hand, is an attempt to dilute the meaning and power forgiveness offers to me. It is a counterfeit—a substitute for forgiveness. It is a decision not to hold a person accountable for his or her actions, but also never to fully release that person from the memories associated with those actions. It is a way to still maintain the memories to extract benefit in the form of guilt from them. It is a way of lying to others and myself about a healing that does not truly exist."

I am shocked and appalled by these thoughts in my head, because it forces me admit I have been playing a foolish game of self-deceit. Though wearing the disguise of the martyr has allowed me to appear *benevolent* and *forgiving*, I have been anything but benevolent or forgiving. I have lived my life wanting and desiring retribution!

As a child, I left Wooster believing I was *owed* something. Like the motivation behind all martyrdom behavior, I wanted payback. I wanted to be compensated for all that I believed I had lost, and I wanted recompense for the love I had given.

This is why, until now, that I could only pardon him and this city, because pardon kept my memories alive. Forgiving him would have relinquished the memories that I desperately needed. Keeping my memories alive allowed me, my stepfather, and this place to remain frozen in time. It was a fictional place where I could create my life through my wounds. It was inevitable that living my life through my wounds could only leave me suspended in an ever present state of "victim."

Maybe it had been a saddened glance from a teacher who had seen my bruises, or from an officer who had to come yet one more time to our home for a domestic disturbance, but somewhere along the way, I had gotten the impression that when a person is a *victim,* they are not responsible or accountable for the events that happen in their life. Somehow I came to believe there are exceptions for victims—they are "special." Living my life through my wounds provided me with sympathy and a way out of the troubling situations of my life—allowing me to remain a victim long after the police had gone, the bruises had healed, and the years had past.

How disillusioned and mistaken I had been all these years, attempting to gain personal power by playing the victim. It all seemed to make sense to me now. Within the walls of my Wooster home, I was taken hostage and my fear had taught me to survive by learning the way of the victim; when I moved away from Wooster, I remained a prisoner by my own choosing. Holding onto my past, I had simply changed the face of my abuser with that of my memories, ensuring my torment would never end. This was a vicious merciless cycle with no end and no healing.

I had managed all these years to keep the victim within me hidden away undetected. All the while, it had become my continuous companion through life. Sitting here now, with its face exposed to me, I can not recall one moment when I could not see the victim's treacherous hand upon my life, or when I did not hear its deceitful voice in my ears. No, it was always present, even at the happiest moments of my life. It whispered viciously, telling me that, "it wouldn't last" or that "I didn't deserve it" or that "in time I would lose this too," and the big one that, "I was a failure."

I could see clearly the terror and confusion that had absorbed my life during my Wooster years, was still absorbing my life today. By not letting go of the memories that I experienced there, I had caused myself to masquerade a broken life. The pain I had experienced as a child was no comparison to the horrid suffering I had caused myself throughout my life by wearing the face of the victim.

As a child, I had been unaware of the beliefs that lay beneath the surface of "pity" a victim seems to gain. Even to the kindest heart, though pity is shown to a victim, they are always seen as defective, broken, and non-repairable. Playing the martyr and the victim was a form of self punishment and self vengeance. They helped me to maintain a belief in hate and guilt, which ultimately ended with me. In this I had been more brutal than any event or memory I held. Creating my life from my wounds, life became something that happened to me and not something that flowed from me. In the end, being a victim only taught me to close my heart to others, to fear them and to want them to fear in return.

"How many relationships have I entered into with these beliefs?" I wonder. I knew the answer is "all of them." I am always fighting an "image" in my mind. My continual conflict with the past makes it certain that I will recreate the same conflict within my future relationships.

Wooster is the place of my origin of thought. It is the place from which I have been basing my life experiences. Inside of my wounds, I held the beliefs that I couldn't trust those in control; people who "love" you lie, and that they can and will physically and emotionally hurt you. Even though I believe love is the only thing anyone wants in life, I left Wooster as a child believing people aren't capable of deeply loving, including me. Though I had lived hundreds—even—thousands of miles away from here, I never escaped these beliefs; Wooster has haunted me my entire life.

However, today is different. Wooster is a catalyst. Returning here, I realize what I have taught myself is not real or reliable—I had been building my life on illusions. I know that having this realization is only the beginning. The power of this lesson is not in the discovery, but in what I will do with this discovery. Having now recognized this face of fear, and how it manifested itself in my life, I wonder, if I can leave it behind or if I had grown so accustomed to its presence in my life that I can not bear to live my life without it.

After some thought, I know this is not a question that can be asked and answered in one quick sweeping moment of my life. No, this is a life question that will require the continuous answering as life's events present themselves to me. I know that I will be answering this question for the rest of my life.

Leaving Wooster behind me, I say to myself,

"Liberty Street is an appropriate name," and I contemplate what opening my heart to freedom will mean for me. For the first time, I understand that I have been an unhealed healer for the entirety of my life. As Wooster becomes smaller and smaller in my driver side mirror, I say out loud these words, "It is time to forget. I am ready to heal."

Thirty Pieces of Silver; Selling-Out

It is early September, and I am tired. My body aches, and at this moment, I am filled with an indescribable agony, silent tears stream down my face, I feel lost. I try to comfort myself with the thought that only 3 months remain that I am mandated to drive. But today, it might as well be 3 years. My days and nights blend together in isolation, it is an endless silence that leaves me feeling desolate, abandoned, forgotten. Each day seems to disappear into the next, and before I know it, weeks have passed. I feel like I have been traveling these roads forever. It is as if lifetimes have come and gone since I entered this big truck. Yet, I carry on; I am unstoppable. I drive on, having conquered the ability to drive, even when the pain inside of me pleads with me to pull over, to stop, to get out. I drive on blinking through my tears.

Arriving at the Petro Truck Stop in Reno, Nevada, I pull into a parking space and turn off my truck. I wait, listening to the CB radio; a woman is singing a bad rendition of the Star Spangle Banner. Other drivers are cursing and yelling at her to shut-up, but she continues to sing. Still sitting in the driver seat, I reach down and turn off the radio, sighing. "This is my life," I say to myself, not with humor but sadness.

I reach for my laundry bag and exit my big truck. Walking toward the door, I feel a strange sensation. Maybe it was the thousands of blinking lights on the billboards and buildings I had passed all day, lighting up the faces of happy winners with the promises that I, too, could be winning millions. Whatever the case, I think, "Why not me? Why are my chances any less likely than another's?" So, after I place my clothes in the washer, into the lion's den I enter.

The casino is dimly lit. The stench of cigarettes and smelly truck drivers permeates the air. All around me, coins are dropping and dinging bells announce the small and large wins of other patrons. I walk through, carefully surveying my surroundings. Which machine to pick is an important question, and I know I need to take my time, because winning *millions* is an important task.

Finding a seat, I pull a ten dollar bill from my pocket and slip it into the nickel slot machine in front of me. A flood of nickels empties into my tray.

I take a deep breath and begin my bargaining. "God," I say, "You know I am not a miser or a selfish person, and I will share my big winnings. First, I will pay my debts and then I will share the remainder with family and friends." That is all I say before picking up a handful of nickels. Slowly, one by one, I drop 3 coins into the slot machine. I pull the handle down gently, while envisioning myself walking away from my truck. The words from an old song written by Johnny Paycheck "Take This Job and Shove It," sounds loudly in my head. It is silly, really. Whoever heard of someone winning a million dollars from a slot machine? Though I have not, that does not stop me from believing in magic. I wait, holding my breath until the spinning stops, revealing to me my winnings—nothing.

I am undeterred. With a two handed coordination I am surprised I possess, I repetitively fed coins into the slot machine. Within minutes, I am nearing the end of my coins. Finally, six coins drop into my tray; this gives me a renewed hope but after a few more meager "wins," my ten dollars is gone. Before I know it, I am caught up in the nonsense desperate people tell themselves: "Perhaps, this is a test? Have a little faith! I have to have a win soon! Just a couple more times and it will all pay off," I say, reaching into my billfold pulling out a twenty dollar bill and slipping it into the slot machine. Smiling, I wait for the 400 nickels to fall into my tray below.

As my twenty dollars begins to disappear like the ten dollars before it into the slot machine, I am no longer playing a game. I am serious, as I watch with intensity, waiting for the spinning wheel to stop. In nervous anticipation, I begin to run my hands over my face and through my hair in-between spins. My skin is hot. I am sweating. Looking down, my hands are covered with a thick black substance. "Yuck! Are the coins really that dirty, or are they coated with some kind of oil?" I wonder. I do not allow this to divert my attention. After all, there is no time to waste; I am deeply mesmerized by the spinning wheel before me.

Down to my last ten nickels, desperation begins to take over when finally my machine lights up and a bell begins to ding. I hit a jack pot! A total of 300 nickels, the equivalent of fifteen dollars, is released into my tray. A renewed hope surges through me and I play on. I hit another jack pot of 30 nickels, a total of one dollar and fifty cents. Again, 30 nickels . . . 30 nickels . . . 10 nickels . . . 10 nickels . . . 6 nickels . . . 0 nickels . . . 0 nickels . . . 0 nickels . . . no more nickels, my twenty dollars is gone.

Reluctantly, I remember my clothes in the washer. I know I need to move them over to the dryer, but I do not want to leave my seat. Rational thinking eludes me; I fear someone might come and take my seat, reaping the benefits from my losses. I wait, until it is not practical to wait.

Finally, getting up, I scold myself, "Good Grief, get a grip!" I walk out of the casino and into the women's restroom to wash my hands before handling my clean clothes. Inside the restroom, I am startled by my own reflection in the mirror. I look frightening. Around my eyes and face I have smeared black grease from the coins. I hardly recognize myself; I am immediately embarrassed. It takes me several minutes to remove all the black from my hands and face. After placing my clothes into the dryer, I walk back through the casino, and I feel relief to see my machine is still vacant. I anxiously sit down, open my billfold, and take out my last twenty dollar bill. I quickly slip it into the change slot.

I begin working with a precision that makes me feel as though I am an extension of the machine. I work expressionlessly. At times, I move faster than the slot machine's ability to read the coins. Those coins are lost to me. Each time the spinning stops, I add 3 more coins and pull the lever.

As the last few coins of my twenty disappear into the slot machine, I no longer hold out hope for a huge win. By this time I only want to regain the fifty dollars I have lost. Instead of millions of dollars, other images move slowly through my mind. I wonder what Amanda will say about my carelessness. I rehearse in my mind telling her, but the thought makes me apprehensive. I know that at first, she will probably not believe me. She will think I am joking, because neither of us gambles, not even for entertainment.

When the spinning finally stops for the last time, I slowly stand up, move away from the slot machine, and walk away. I am broke, having spent my toll and weigh ticket money for the rest of the week. I groan inwardly. Walking directly to the ATM machine, I withdraw forty dollars, place it in my billfold, and immediately walk out of the casino; listening to the sounds of coins dropping and bells dinging announcing the small and large wins of other patrons.

After retrieving my laundry from the dryer, I retreat to my big truck. Lying in my bunk, I recall the events of the day, especially those inside the casino. I think about my mother's luck at gambling, winning thousands of dollars playing slot machines in Reno, Nevada. I recall my youngest brother, who won seventy-five thousands dollars on one lotto ticket. "What's wrong with me?" I wonder, in self pity and remorse. I lay there for hours feeling like a "victim"; I convince myself that I am the unwanted bastard child of the Universe.

The pain in my chest is so intense that I think my heart will burst; it is only at this moment that I can begin to hear the counsel of my soul. "Winning money is not what I need. In fact, there is not enough money in the world to heal the wound that aches inside of me." I want to argue this point but I do not, because I know on some cellular level I have held the belief that money is the answer to all of my problems. I know that though the casino experience is an isolated event in form it is not isolated in intent. I have been seeking money as a means to fulfill me, or to reach my goals my entire life. "Isn't that how I ended up in this big truck?" I ask myself.

Sitting in my truck watching drivers entering and exiting the casino, I know I am not alone with my beliefs. There are hundreds, thousands, even millions, of people who believe or have believed the same lies about money in their own lives. "How sad," I think to myself, "how sad for us all."

I realize, that if I had "won," it would have only perpetuated the myth that money is the answer, further promoting gambling as a viable means to solving financial problems and reaching one's goals. The reality is that there are far too many people with financial problems and far too few in comparison who will ever win the lotto, or slots, or any other type of gambling game. "Gambling can not be the answer or the solution," I tell myself.

Though intellectually it is easy to understand, it is much harder to accept this as truth, because all of my life—I wanted money to be the answer. I wanted it to change my world. I did not want to accept that the problems which plagued my heart could not, would not be swept away by a larger bank account! In my mind, I form my argument. "It is so unfair! If I had enough money I would not be in this truck! I would be living a different life; the one I was intended to live!" I think angrily as the tears for the second time today stream down my face.

But then, I hear the questioning from a depth I had forgotten existed within me. "Would I? Would I, really?" my soul asks.

I do not answer quickly. Instead, I remain quiet. "Would I? Would I, really" these words repeat in my head. My breath becomes deep and heavy, and I tremble as if I am cold, but I am not cold. Nevertheless, I can not stop trembling. "What does all of this mean? What is happening to me?" I wonder.

I anxiously look for a distraction anything to take my mind away from what I am experiencing at this moment. I reach for my log book. Holding it in my hands I think of the names I have heard other drivers use to describe this book. Many call it their "coloring book"; I choose to affectionately refer to it as, "My book of lies." I open it up to record the fictitious events of my day. "My book of lies," I say out-loud to myself as I begin to draw my lines on the graph. I feel tightness in my throat and chest. It is hard for me to swallow. My hands still tremble, and my heart races, I slam my log book shut. "I am a sell-out," I say to myself. I am shocked and disgusted as if seeing my lies for the first time. I weep deep and sorrowfully. "I am swimming in a world of materialism that is drowning me!" I cry.

At that moment, I want to hide, to disappear; I do not want to accept the truth about myself. I do not want to believe I am capable of selling-out. "Not me, the one with high morals! Not me, the one who is constantly preaching about how others are raping and pillaging our Earth! Not me, the one who is quick to judge Corporate America as a thief, hoarder, and exploiter!" I tell myself.

"At least they sold-out for millions," I think cynically. I think about these many months on the road. I had convinced myself that I did what I did because I had to. I had to for Amanda, because it was not fair to place the entire financial burden on her, and I did it for Paradise because it was what was expected of me. "I had no choice!" I had told myself over and over, but that was just another lie I had told myself to justify my actions. Once again, I recognize how I have pretended to be the victim, but I am no victim here. This was never about Paradise, or Amanda. Nor was I the bastard child of a cruel Universe that was ignoring and rejecting me. I did what I did for myself. When I compromised my integrity I did so because of *my own beliefs* about finances. Over the years, I had looked at Amanda's income and then at my own, and I felt embarrassed and ashamed because I did not think I contributed enough to our household in comparison. It was hard to admit to myself that what I had done I did for my own greed, no one else's. Yes, we needed me to work full-time, but I was the one who decided to drive a truck because I had been told it paid better than my social work positions.

I attempt to console myself. I search my mind for reassurances that this trucking experience is the first time I have compromised myself, but there is no comfort for me. I know the truth, and I can not reject it so easily now. Looking back, I can see hundreds of times I compromised myself because of my belief about not having enough or being enough.

I remembered the many times I had sold out when it came to money. I remembered arguments I had with my sons about how much something "cost" and other money related issues. Now, in this somber moment, I ask myself, "What was I teaching them?"

"Sadly, I have role-modeled for them that money

is more important than people, relationships, or family," I say shaking my head in disbelief. "I taught them all of this because I was fearful that I would not have enough money to cover the phone bill, electric bill, the house payment, or food expenses?" I ask as a question, but intend for it to be a protective statement.

"No, I have taught them these things because I have been greedy. I am motivated by the greed of *what I want*," I say honestly.

As difficult as it is to accept, I know this is true. I know that when I decide I want something, I can surround myself with a thousand reasons why I need to have it, by aligning myself with people and situations that will justify and support what I want. I think about how I cringe when I hear others say that, "every person has a price." I had always secretly and arrogantly said to myself, "not me." Now, I know those days are gone. I have to ask myself, "How much? For how much am I willing to sell-out? What is the price I accept for my soul?"

"Mere pennies," I say bitterly, "that amount to a few dollars and cents on a paycheck at the end of each week." I vow from this night forward, I will never willingly or knowingly lie on my log book again.

I recognize my belief in lack, and selling-out is costing me my life. As I lay in my bunk and cry myself to sleep, I have one last thought. It is about Judas and how he has been mocked throughout the centuries for selling-out for only *thirty pieces of silver*; when in retrospect, it cost him *everything*.

"Isn't the price always *thirty pieces of silver?*" I mumble to myself as I drift off to sleep.

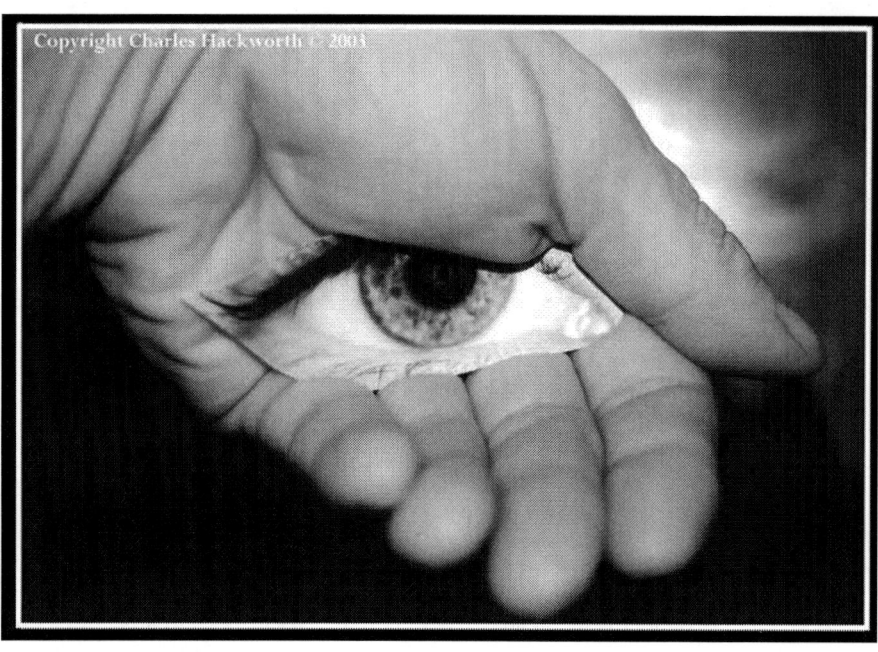

When No One is Watching

I am traveling east in heavy traffic on Interstate 40 across Oklahoma. As I near an onramp, I can see a string of cars are attempting to merge. I slow down to 50 mph, allowing four of the cars to safely merge in front of me. However, a fifth motorist driving an SUV speeds up and tries to squeeze between me and the fourth car now positioned in front of me. There is no place for me to go. Heavy traffic in the left lane makes a lane change impossible. Even if I slam on my brakes, it will take too long for me to stop because the merge ramp is ending. The motorist in the SUV slows down. I watch as his car seems to stand still as my truck begins to pull away from him. He merges directly behind me.

I remain alert as I observe this same motorist in my driver-mirror swerving toward the center line, attempting to force his way into the bumper to bumper traffic flow of the left passing lane. Finally, after several failed efforts he is successful. Slowly, each car that passes me on the left brings the SUV closer to me.

As the motorist in the SUV nears my truck, I can see that mere inches separate him from the bumper of the car in front. It is as if he is attempting to force the other driver out of his way. I have a strong sensation in my gut that he is going to do something unsafe. I can tell by the way he is driving that he is mad that he was unable to merge onto the onramp when he wanted. I take my foot off the throttle and begin to slow down in anticipation. As he begins to pass me on the left, he swerves into my lane, squeezing between me and the driver in front of me, barely missing my front bumper while waving his middle finger prominently at me. With no safe following distance between us, he taps hard on his brakes. Fortunately, I had followed my gut and had slowed down in expectation. I respond by braking hard while maintaining my lane. I pray that I will stop in time as his break lights disappear from my view.

Thankfully, four wheelers (that is what truckers call cars and small trucks) can slow down and speed up faster than a big truck. As quickly as he tapped his breaks, he accelerates. His actions, coupled with my braking, keeps me from driving on-top of his SUV, smashing him and his passenger. As quickly

When No One is Watching

as he entered my lane, he is gone, swerving in and out of the two lanes of traffic.

My heart still pounds as he fades out of my sight. My legs tremble. "I need to get out of this truck," I think to myself. My second thought is, "It is all in a days work." I know this is true. As a professional driver, it is my job to anticipate drivers who are careless, suffering from road rage, or who are inattentive. I experience near disasters everyday from other motorists, debris in the road, severe weather conditions, and an assortment of other hazardous driving conditions. This incident that lasted nearly 5-10 minutes was nothing unusual.

After a moment like this, I always feel the need to share it, but there is no one here. I am alone in my truck; I have no one watching me, no one congratulating me, or cheering me onward. Nearly ninety percent of my time on the road, there is no one aware of what is happening to me but me. Sometimes after these near misses, I call Amanda to share it with her, but usually she is in a meeting or otherwise unavailable. By the time we talk that evening, I am so tired and so many other things have happened, that it no longer seems important enough to retell—the story just becomes lost in the history of my life and this makes me sad.

Most days, like today, it is my experience and mine alone. As I drive onward, I remember the words my trainer, Edward, said to me when I was in Green Bay, "If you want a job where you will be recognized for a job well done or you want to be acknowledged for the work you do—then this is the wrong profession, because you will never get it in this industry." I know now that he was telling me the truth.

I reach for my cell phone and call Amanda, but it rings to her voice mail. I sigh. "Oh, well," I say, "it doesn't matter."

"That is a lie," I tell myself. It does matter to me; I am disappointed that I have no one to tell. "Why do I think the things that happen with me only matter when I have an audience or someone congratulating me?" I wonder. Yet, what I really want to know, but had not dared to ask until now, is, "Why do I believe *I do not matter* unless someone else knows about my accomplishments or my achievements?" I ask sadly.

I can feel the sting of tears in my eyes. I clench my teeth and breathe deeply, trying to suppress the emotions these questions begin to stir in me. I want to shrug it off, to forget I have even posed these questions. "Why do I have to be so insecure?" I ask myself angrily. "And why do I have to get so upset over it?" I continue, becoming even angrier with myself.

I am upset because I know that somewhere, buried deep in the layers of those questions, hides a motive that I do not like about myself. It is like a thorn in my side and I hate it's chaffing, but I would rather deal with that than the truth it hides from me. I view this thorn as a weakness. "Praise junkies" is what I call people who need reassurance and recognition for doing what they ought to do. I had boldly declared myself not a part of that club, but, inwardly, how could I deny that I secretly desire recognition, too. "How else can I explain my actions? What else can be driving my need to have someone acknowledge my accomplishments?" I ask myself. "Perfection," is the only word that enters my mind. "Perfection?" I say, bewildered. I know I am not perfect! What does perfection have to do with . . ." I stop myself mid-thought. It has everything to do with it. To me, perfection is not about a performance. My life is not a recital for the masses, in many ways it is more complex than that. Perfection for me is about being a *good* person. I have to report my *goodness* so others will know I am a *good* person; because I fear that otherwise they will not know it, because secretly I doubt it about myself.

That is why I feel I need to tell someone about my near crashes, and how I managed to maneuver myself to safety. I am a *good* driver, therefore, a *good* person. This is why I need to explain the hardships I am having out on the road to my friends, so they can think about how *determined* and *persevering* I am. *Determined* and *persevering* people are *good*. I have to be *perfect* because I want to be *good*. But it has never been enough to just do it perfectly—I have to share it. Someone else has to know about it too; only when someone else confirms my so-called *goodness* can I believe it is true. Secretly, I hold the belief that anything I do is never *good* enough. The praise and recognition I seek is not to boost my ego, but to keep me alive, to allow me to believe there is something worthwhile in me.

Realizing this, every action of my entire life becomes suspect. "How much of the life I am living is the life I want, and not the life whereby others will bestow upon me the crown of *goodness* for living?"

Suddenly, every benevolent act I have ever done seems tainted and flawed. I admit to myself that this is a hard realization to grasp, while I continue to cling to an unhealthy and an unrealistic image of spirituality that seems synonymous with *perfection*. Yet there is nothing sacred about this image, and for all of my efforts to be *good*, in my mind, it has only led me further from God. At this moment, sitting in my big truck, I am lonelier than I have ever been in my life. I know I can never trust this image of myself again. Looking into my life that has been a façade, my *goodness* is nothing more than a self righteous garment I wear to impress, to draw others to me.

Regardless of how I look at it, the "praise junkies" and I are twins. It does not matter that our motives *appear* to be different. It is all self-serving and manipulative. "Why do I need to seek my approval from others so desperately? Why?" I cry.

"Because I have so little for myself," is the answer that comes.

There it is. The answer I have been seeking. Desiring approval and recognition is not something *bad,* I had just misunderstood it. Approval is not something I can extract from others, nor is it something I earn by my *good* works. These methods only cleverly shroud my self-hate, and cause me to embark on a long meaningless search where I will never find it—outside of me.

As the weeks pass, I learn to speak less and less about the events that happen to me. I accept them, learn from them, and move on from them. Each day, I become less and less concerned about others approving or disapproving of my actions or the life I live. It is through all of this that I come to understand one of the most powerful revelations of my life: The closest I will ever be to God is when no one else is watching. My purest thoughts and words will be the ones no one will ever hear, and when there is no one whom I want to impress listening or watching. Those are my moments of true communion. Those are the moments when I am the most alive. Today, I am learning to love the silence.

The Face of the Drifter; The Cruelest Form of Abuse

It was 3:00 a.m. when I heard a knock at the door. Startled, I jumped to my feet, grabbing my glasses from the nightstand beside my bunk. I slid open the curtain on the driver side window and groggily peered out to stare into a woman's face. She looked to be in her late 30's or early 40's and she had shoulder length blonde hair. Her face looked tired, and looking into her eyes I knew she had seen better days. She was leaning against my door, moving her mouth and jaw in a sucking motion like she was gasping for air, and waved her hands in a gesture for me to open my door. I rolled the window down instinctively, without caution.

"What do you want?" I asked.

"Oh, sorry about that, I am looking for someone else, a friend of mine, his truck looked like yours," she said as she jumped off the steps of my big truck. I watched her walk to the blue big truck parked beside my orange Paradise truck. "She must be color blind," I said, laughing to myself. I watched her for several minutes go from truck to truck knocking on each door.

I closed the curtain and sleepily sat down on my bunk, rubbing my eyes. I knew the woman who woke me had been what is referred to by most drivers as a "Lot Lizard" (a prostitute that works the truck stops and rest areas looking for truckers). I shrugged off her uninvited visit and went to sleep, unaffected.

The following evening, I was waiting at a grocery warehouse in Houston, TX. Around 10:30 p.m. I received a knock on my door. I slowly pulled my body upright and strained to see through blurry vision. I had fallen to sleep while I waited for Security to contact me over my CB that it was my turn to back into a dock. I immediately jumped to my feet, "Just a minute," I called out. Initially, I worried I must have slept so soundly that I missed the dispatch's call. I ran my fingers threw my hair, and tucked my shirt evenly before pulling open the curtain above my driver's door.

A tall thin middle-aged man stood peering in my window. I rolled my window down a few inches. "Good evening miss. My name is Jerome and I am homeless. I am out here trying to better myself by working, because I want to get off these streets. A lot of the drivers out here help me out by allowing me to shine their rims for only $5.00 each," he said smiling.

I sat there motionless for a moment or two, just

looking at him. His eyes were familiar to me. "Yes, Jerome, I remember you from 3 months ago. That is when I was here the last time," I said, annoyed that he did not have the consciousness to know he had already used this line on me before.

His expression went blank, "Oh, yes, I remember you, too. How are you doing?"

"I am tired, Jerome, and I do not want my rims cleaned tonight."

"Miss, I understand it's late, but do you have any spare change you could give me because I'm so hungry? I have not eaten all day."

I had no way of knowing if he was homeless, but I was certain that he had no intention of giving up this gig, because begging had become as much his job as driving had become mine. I reached into the cup holder on my dash where I kept my toll money. "Here you go Jerome," I said handing him some change. "I am really tired and need some sleep could you please keep watch over my truck and make sure no one else knocks on my truck waking me?" I asked.

"Yes, I will. No one will bother you. I promise you. Thank you, miss, and you have a good night."

"You are welcome and you have a good night too, Jerome," I said as I rolled up my window. I closed the curtain and crawled back into my bunk, but I found it difficult to sleep. It seemed strange to me that two nights in a row I would be awakened by similar situations. There was something about Jerome and the woman that bothered me, something about looking into their eyes that made me sad.

"They're lost souls, drifters," I said to myself, attempting to label or categorize them so I could find the appropriate "feeling" response. Though I tried, I was unable to get them out of my mind. I had seen the sadness and the pain in their eyes, and it troubled me.

I thought about all the prostitutes, homeless men, and addicts I had encountered over the months as a driver. I found myself recalling many of the homeless individuals I had worked with in Phoenix as a pastor, but not only there. I thought about many of the addicts and the homeless individuals I had worked with throughout my lifetime, and I could vividly see their faces, their eyes, their tears.

Until that moment, I had never realized our similarities. I had always viewed these individuals as separate, apart from me. They were the "drifters," they were the "lost" ones, not me. All of these years, I had been arrogantly mistaken, believing I was but a humble supporter reaching out to them. In a moment of clarity those thoughts ceased, vanishing forever from my mind; I realized that when I had stared into their eyes I had always seen my own reflection. These people and I, we were all drifters. To my dismay, I realized that my attraction to the homeless, the addict, the *lost*, the *drifter*, was nothing more than my misguided attempts to heal my own pain, my own longings, my own soul. Like Jonah, we had all been seeking a way to the city of Tarshish, but God intervened and we ended up in the belly of the whale instead.

By this time in my Jonah experience, I

understood that the road to Tarshish was a figment of my mind's imagination. Tarshish was symbolic, a name of a place I sought to escape from God, the Spirit dwelling within me, and from my own personal gifts. Thankfully, a journey away from God was impossible, because God encompasses all of life; there is no place I could run where God is not present.

There is no mention of how long Jonah drifted among the waves before he was swallowed by the whale. The author only tells us how long he drifted in the belly of the whale (3 days and 3 nights), before he agreed to go to Nineveh. How long had I drifted before being swallowed by this big truck? How many days, weeks, or years?" I asked myself.

"Every bit of it!" I answered.

I achingly admitted that my life had been full of endless seeking, but I was never able to find my niche. I had unsuccessfully tried more careers than anyone I knew, none of which had ever completely satisfied me; I had never come to terms with my own desires. Never living up to my full potential, wearing the face of the drifter, was the cruelest expression of my self-hate. Climbing into this big truck had been just another manifestation of my own relentless self-abuse, a way to punish myself. Like Jonah's whale, my big truck had no destination. Symbolically, I was a gypsy having no home, no roots, and no meaningful connection with others.

Sitting there, I understood that Jonah, Jerome, and I were not different. We had each become beggars even as we sat before the banquet table of life. We coveted the plates of others, and rejected what was set before us. Our lives became reduced to pleading, sobbing, and clawing at our gnawing stomachs as we watched, hoping for a fallen crust of bread to drop from another plate that would sustain us—giving our lives substance.

"What was this fallen crust of bread I waited for? Did such a crust even exist?" I wondered.

I contemplated Jonah's experience and his search for his fallen "crust." I thought about how extreme God's request must have seemed to Jonah; I understood why it forced him to question everything that he had been taught or believed to be true about himself and others, but most importantly, about God.

In Jonah's world, a Universal God (a God who could exist and be shared equally among all people) did not exist. Nor did a god exist who accepted equally all of humanity. As a Hebrew, Jonahs', "God" only existed in the form of "Adonai," or as "YHWH" who had selectively chosen certain tribes of people to adore and others to despise. Therefore, going to Nineveh made no sense to Jonah, because it was not populated with Hebrews. Nineveh was a land filled with Assyrians who did not worship *YHWH*. To make matters worse, the Assyrians were among the most feared people of Jonah's era. They were known as skilled warriors, ruthless and barbaric to their enemies. In Jonah's eyes, the Assyrians were heathens, and held no redemptive qualities; he loathed them.

Even if Jonah had not disliked the people of

Nineveh, how could he justify his behavior to other Hebrews? They would have certainly questioned Jonah's motives for extending God beyond their religious traditions. Jonah concluded that there were other more worthy things he could do with his life. Going to Nineveh, the home of his enemy was not one of them. He could see no value in what God asked of him; he concluded that going to Nineveh was unimportant.

While thinking on these things, I realized what Jonah had figured out long ago. The "crust" that he waited for to drop in his lap could not be found on his meaningless trip to Tarshish, nor could he find it by remaining in the belly of the whale. This meant Jonah could no longer disregard his own place at the banquet table. He had to release his desire to eat from the crumbs and accept his own plate. Therefore, he must go to Nineveh.

I did not know what Jerome's crust was nor did I know what it was for any of the hundreds of drifters I had been acquainted with during my lifetime, but I did know mine. As far back as I could remember, I had possessed the uncanny knack for looking out into the world around me and seeing what others seemed only vaguely aware was there, if at all. Not being an extrovert by nature, yet feeling compelled to share my thoughts, I did not know what to do with the feelings that welled up inside of me. This often left me feeling odd, peculiar, or like I did not *fit*. Not knowing what else to do, I began to write, and a whole new world opened up for me as I expressed my thoughts through short stories, plays, and poems.

When I was eleven years old, I visited a Church of Christ Church and had a profound life altering experience with God which resulted in my deciding to be baptized. An hour later when I returned home with my hair still wet, my mother inquired as to what had happened to me. When I explained to her that I had been baptized she replied, "We are Catholic." I was stunned. Instinctively, I knew that being Catholic or Church of Christ had nothing to do with God. A few months later, I decided I would become a minister. Not in the traditional sense, but through my writing and missionary work.

From this point on, the focus of my writing began to change. I often felt compelled to write about how I experienced God in my life. By the age of twelve, I attempted to write my first book. It was simply entitled "Love" and it was about how I saw God in every blade of grass, every tree, every flower, every animal, and every person I met. The words flowed out of me like music, and I was never happier than when I was expressing God through my written words.

After I had completed a few chapters, I decided to share it with an adult (my stepfather's younger sister, my aunt by marriage). When I asked her about it, she seemed speechless. She acknowledged only that she had read it but nothing more. I judged her reaction to mean that I had misinterpreted God. I discarded the book and began again attempting a more acceptable approach to God, but in time I lost interest, because I was writing about a god I did not know. Nevertheless, I did continue to write, about life and my experiences.

Though my friends enjoyed my poems and short stories, the adults in my life seldom did. My friends seemed to be able to see beyond my grammar and spelling errors, to grasp the meaning of my writings. My teachers, on the other hand, were not so forgiving, usually returning my papers covered in red ink and with a grade that was barely passing, if passing at all. This did not deter me; I continued to write.

It was during my freshman year that I began to think about publishing my writings. I wanted to share my stories and ideas with the world. I did not know how to undertake such a task. After much thought, I decided to take one of my best writing pieces to a teacher I admired. He was an English teacher at my high school. I had never personally had him as an instructor, but I had heard many positive comments about him from other students.

One day, I went to him and discussed my ambitions and I gave him a writing sample of my work, and then waited to hear from him. I waited for a week. I would pass him in the hallways, but he would hurry by me on his way to class, never noticing me. I continued to wait. I am not certain how long I waited, but at the time it felt like an eternity.

Finally, one day I stopped him and inquired about my writing. Standing there in the hallway with my heart pounding, smiling I waited with exuberance and anticipation. I wanted to hear him tell me how moving and compelling my writing had been and that by all means I should continue to pursue writing as a career. However, those words never came from his lips. Instead, in a tone that was matter of fact, he told me, "Your writing is distracting, too full of grammatical errors."

Okay, so my grammar wasn't that great. No one had to tell me I had been a mediocre student, I knew this already. In fact, it was common knowledge. But, was my writing compelling? Was it intriguing? Those were the questions I wanted answered. "Do you think I have a chance to be a writer someday if I improved the grammar stuff? Should I continue to write?" I asked eagerly. I was unaware of the traffic and voices that surrounded us in the hallway, and at that moment, the only thing that existed were the words he spoke to me. That was over twenty-eight years ago, and though I can not remember verbatim his exact words, I do remember the gist of them. "There are a lot of people who want to be writers . . . few will ever become published. . . . It is a very competitive . . . difficult field. . . . It would be better for you to seek another profession. . . ."

"But, if I were to make the changes necessary to make it grammatically correct, would it be a good story? Would it be ok then? Could I be a writer, then?" I asked fearfully, nearly choking on each word.

He looked at me and seemed to be searching for the right words to say to me, "Joyce you are not a writer. You should look into another profession. You are just not a writer."

I do not remember anything else about that day, except that I was speechless. I felt as if my entire world had stopped, and crumbled at my feet. That day, I decided that I would no longer listen to the writer inside of me; she had been a waste of my time. I banished her to the deepest recesses of my being, and forbade her to freely speak to me again.

I did all of this because someone, I did not even know, whose opinion others had valued and respected, had implied that I was finished or that I had no talent. Though later in high school and in college there were other teachers who held a different opinion, and who often encouraged me to further explore my writing abilities, regardless of how good their words made me feel, I never allowed myself to take their words seriously. Yet, every teacher who ever seemed to disregard or find fault with my words, those teachers I remembered well.

As the years passed, I hated allowing others to read my writings. I grudgingly wrote for school assignments and I wrestled with how I would fulfill my desire to minister if not through my writing. The most logical solution was to become a traditional minister. For years, I drifted in and out of church organizations attempting to find the *right* one, before joining a deeply fundamentalist organization. By my early twenties, I had finished Bible College and was ministering and teaching within that organization. I was also coming to terms with the reality that I was a lesbian, and this only made my search more complicated. In the end, my Theological degree, evangelistic work, and all ministerial accomplishments would be stripped from me. According to that organization and many church traditions I was *unfit* to minister in any capacity, because being a lesbian was banned unacceptable. Though religion seemed to reject me, I never stopped loving God or desiring to connect spiritually with others.

After being ex-communicated, I desperately wanted to keep my religious voice alive. I picked up my pen and paper and for the first time in over a decade I decided to write. However, my attempt at writing failed. I became discouraged convincing myself that no publishing company or church group would be interested in reading the words of a lesbian minister.

That is when I decided to enroll in a state college. Years passed but by the time I graduated with my degree in Sociology, I once again found myself longing for the ministry, winding up as the pastor of my own organization. It was a wonderful experience, and though it was different from any church I had experienced, it echoed the traditional role of pastor. It was during those years that I realized I did not want to minister—not in the traditional sense, because it limited me. I was uncomfortable standing before people lecturing. I wanted to connect with them, and how could I connect with others when I was positioned above them? I wanted to share ideas with others, not instruct them how to live. I wanted to inspire myself and others to awaken from the sleeping existence most of us called our lives. But the details I wanted others to workout for themselves. I wanted them to seek their own salvation, to dictate and design their own lives. At a time when the church was growing and it seemed success was evident, I walked away from it all; I realized that I was limited by the general interpretation given to ministry by myself and others.

Afterwards, two years would pass and I would find it difficult, having no outlet, no forum to express my thoughts. One morning I turned on my computer and for the first time in years I began to seriously write; I had no work project, no church message to prepare, no school assignment to write. I simply wrote because I wanted to. However, I kept it bridled, restrained. This was no free verse writing; this writing was careful and deliberate. I put my thoughts neatly and orderly into a series of workshops. I would go on to share those workshops with hundreds of people. Sharing those workshops only intensified the longing that already existed within me to write, but I rejected this longing until finally I ended up in the belly of this big truck.

It was not until now that I truly understood why I had held onto the words spoken by an individual nearly 28 years earlier. It was for the same reasons I had held onto so many other self destructive words from others over the years. It has been a central theme not only throughout this book, but throughout my life. I accepted their words because *I did not trust* the beating of my own heart. *I did not trust* the wisdom of my own intuition, and *I did not trust* the voice of my own soul. So many years were spent longing, searching, crying out, wishing for life to end, but afraid of it ending; somehow I knew that I was not living the life I was intended to live. I hated my life because I believed it had no meaning, because it existed by breathing the stale air I called life.

Inside of me was the heart of a writer. She had always existed, always lived. She was there every step of the way, calling me, asking me to speak to myself and others through my writing, but I denied her presence. I pretended she was not there. Instead of living and expressing myself as I knew instinctively, I was made to become a shadow in my own life. I was going through the motions of life, but not experiencing it.

Suddenly, looking out the window of this big truck was different for me. I could feel a weight lifting from me. Decisions I had made did not seem so damning. Directions I had taken in my life seemed to make sense. It was not that I was a failure. The problem was that I had been approaching life backwards. I had been trying to fulfill my natural purpose by going the opposite way down a one-way street. This is why I appeared to be sometimes "on" and sometime "off" in my life. This endless cycle caused me to become frustrated, disinterested, and depressed. At times, I believed "if only I worked harder, then I would be successful." Now, I could see it so clearly; it had nothing to do with "working harder." It had everything to do with focusing my intentions on my life's purpose. Otherwise, I would continue to walk disconnected through life. I had been living my life groping blindly, living life behind a curtain, a veil that separated me from my truth.

At this moment, I knew for the first time that I was not alone in my Jonah experience; the world was filled with millions like me. I could see the faces of so many friends, family, and acquaintances I had known that stopped short of their dreams, becoming the art critic instead of the artist, or those who became the construction worker instead of the architect, contractor, or designer. Like me, they had never been satisfied, always criticizing the work of others, but too afraid to step out and live, believing instead that we needed to settle. So, settle we did into our nice, neat, worlds of anguish and pain.

Looking out on an empty parking lot, I knew that though the world seemed to be the same, for me, it had changed. From that moment onward, I knew I would write again. I felt my voice re-emerging, and I knew the first story I would write would be the story about *Jonah and me*. I was no longer concerned with who would read it, because it did not matter. I would write it because it is who I was, who I am; it is part of the reason I exist. It is my purpose to share it and to allow others to do with it what they wanted. This is my gift. I would no longer live my life under the mistaken assumption that what God had asked of me was unimportant.

That night as I closed my eyes to sleep, I knew it was time . . . time to leave my big truck. I could walk away now. Nineveh was waiting for me.

Going Back to the Whale

On December 15th I walked into my company's St. Louis, Missouri office with my truck keys and fuel card in hand. I gave them to one of the managers, smiled, and walked out the door. I could freely walk away without reprisal; I had fulfilled my commitment. As I stepped outside, I took a deep breath and looked around me. It was a beautiful winter's day and for the first time in over a year I was going home with the intention to stay.

As I walked away, I had every confidence that the doors were going to open for me. I had no reason to suspect otherwise. During the six weeks since I had given my notice, everything else in my life seemed synchronized with a divine order to it. Amanda accepted a new position as a Human Resources Director for a company located in Kansas City, Missouri. We had already purchased a home just to the north of Kansas City. The holidays were nearing. Our sons were coming to visit, and my mother had accepted our invitation to come to live in our home. My life seemed to be going well. All I needed was a "job" and I was confident I would find one. Since October, I had mailed out over 100 resumes into the Kansas City area.

Somehow, in my exuberance I had completely undermined the *Nineveh experience.* For the past year, my entire focus had been on the challenges associated with climbing out of the *whale.* I had mistakenly convinced myself that becoming an expert on being *swallowed up* was somehow the end of the story and not its beginning. Upon leaving my *whale* experience, I had agreed to write my book, the book I had been putting off writing my entire life. I planned to keep this commitment. Having kept a journal since the first day of my training, I had already begun forming chapters from my notes. However, I had my own priorities and agenda on how I would accomplish this. Basically, I would write in my spare time after my other responsibilities were met.

I had forgotten about Jonah's negative attitude as he walked the streets of Nineveh. I had forgotten about how he determined to do things his way, delivering a message of doom and destruction to the people instead of a Universal message of God's love. At that time, he did not know how to separate the god of his childhood and religion from the God of his personal experience that was leading him beyond what those around him could conceive. Likewise, I could not fathom another alternative for how things could unfold in my life. Amanda and I had expenses and debts we owed. I had to have an income. "How could we make it otherwise? Amanda's wages are not enough," I would repetitively say to myself.

As the pile of rejection letters grew daily, I fretted over my decision to leave the big truck. "What was I thinking?" I scolded myself. "How could I quit without having another job?" As the days passed, I frantically searched the newspapers and on the internet for jobs. I became less and less choosey; applying for jobs I did not want. Yet, even this did not stop the rejection letters.

Who in their right mind after climbing out of the *belly of a whale* would go searching for it again and when it was found would pry open the jaws of the beast and climb back in? It would seem only the insane, deranged, or twisted, but that is exactly what I did. After being unemployed only 2 weeks, I feared the worst and did the unthinkable: I accepted a driving position with another trucking company. I had fooled myself into believing that because it was a smaller company with only 300 employees that my experience would be different. I chose to accept the unpleasant known over the ambiguous unknown.

Assigned the oldest truck in the fleet, I shrugged my shoulders and reluctantly went to work. On my second day as a driver, my truck's engine had frozen due to the cold temperatures. I dismissed this omen as something that was normal during the winter months, though I had not experienced this last winter.

I continued onward, and at 11:30 p.m. that night in Cambria, Wisconsin I made a wrong turn onto a dead end road directly beside the factory where I was to deliver. As I attempted to back out of this situation, my left tandem (back trailer tires) became lodged in a ditch, leaving me straddling both sides of the road. By 2:00 a.m., thanks to a young woman named Rhonda and a one hundred and seventy-five dollar tow bill, I was out of the ditch sitting in front of my customer's gate. Also in hand was a one hundred fifty dollar ticket complements of a deputy from the local sheriffs department.

Two days later, (day four on the job) a D.O.T. (Department of Transportation) Officer "shut me down" (stopped me) at a weigh station for being overweight. I had been through weigh stations thousands of times, but I had never been overweight. However, my new employer's policy instructed me not to weigh loads less than 45,000 pounds. The $8.00 to $9.00 dollars it cost to ensure the loads appropriate weight distribution was costing the company an additional $50,000.00 a year. I had questioned this rational during orientation, stating that I felt it was dangerous. However, I was told this was protocol. I asked if I would be reimbursed if I opted to weigh the load. I was told, "NO!" Therefore when my invoice read 44,000 pounds I did not go to a truck stop to weigh it. Unfortunately, the customer had loaded additional weight causing my total load weight to exceed 50,000 pounds. This was a $1,000.00 violation, which created a strain on my relationship with certain individuals in our Safety Department.

As if my first week was not going badly enough, my truck's heater did not work properly. Whenever I stopped at night to rest, my truck would either shut off completely or would blow cold air, causing me to wake up freezing after one or two hours. It was not uncommon to wake up unable to feel my toes or fingers. When I stopped at the company shop to have a mechanic check it, they were always too busy to fix my truck. I continued to drive for three weeks through the states of Wisconsin, Minnesota, Iowa, and Missouri with no heat when I stopped to take my break. I found this particularly frustrating since this was one the coldest winters these states had experienced in several years, with temperatures often below zero.

I pushed myself daily, often exceeding my legal hours of service in an attempt to keep myself warm, because my heater only worked when my truck was in motion. I was exhausted. I laid in my bunk convulsing from the cold until every muscle in my body ached. When the cold became unbearable, I would climb back into the driver seat and begin to drive, pulling over only when I became too tired to stay awake.

As each day passed, I was becoming more sleep deprived and disgruntled by what I considered irresponsible requests for me to drive my truck, regardless of the safety hazards to myself or the public. By the end of week three, I experienced what I mistakenly thought to be my breaking point. The night dispatcher had demanded that I drive my truck with a known Flex Pipe leak, which is a leak allowing carbon monoxide to seep into my cab. The following morning, looking out of my driver window, I believed I was being given more than an opportunity to see barren frozen mounds of snow and thick dead layers of ice that covered the parking lot were I sat. At that moment, I was seeing the barrenness and inevitable death of my own soul. I was dying out here. If not physically, I certainly was emotionally. "Why would anyone willing climb back into the belly of a *whale,* especially when they recognized it was a whale?" I asked myself. Without calling Amanda to discuss it and without thinking about the ramifications, I decided to quit. I gave my two week notice.

I would like to say that was the end of my *swallowed up* experience, but it was not. That same day, the Transportation Manager met with me to discuss my reasons for wanting to quit. During our meeting, he assigned me a newer truck. I gladly switched. However, I told him I was not making any promises that I would remain an employee. Nevertheless, I was enticed by a newer truck and with empty assurances that "we" (the company and I) had gotten off to a "bad beginning".

Over the next two weeks, Amanda and I spoke often about my future. We both agreed I needed to quit driving, but how I would supplement our household income seemed to baffle us both. I kept my fingers crossed, and prayed for a miracle, but when my two weeks had passed and I did not have another job offer, I decided to extend for one more week. I have no doubt that my fear would have caused me to continue extending week by week until another month, or year would have passed. That is, if the events that occurred at the end of that extended week had not happened.

I was to make a simple delivery. I was to drop off a loaded trailer and pick up an empty one. I had performed this function hundreds of times, and it was routine. Yet, when I arrived at the customer's location, I was asked by the customer to remove an empty trailer from the dock, and to replace it with the loaded trailer I had brought to deliver. This entailed unhooking from my existing loaded trailer, hooking to the empty trailer against the dock and pulling it away from the door, parking it, unhooking from it, and then re-hooking to the loaded trailer. Then I needed to back the loaded trailer against the dock and then unhook from it, leaving it there. I would then re-hook to the empty trailer I had pulled away from the dock and parked. All of this would take some time in the 5 degree Wisconsin weather.

I dropped my loaded trailer with ease, but then the problems began. The empty trailer I needed to hookup had sat against the dock for more than 10 days, according to the customer. Upon inspecting, I found the wheel chocks and tires were frozen into the ice. My only recourse at the time was to hammer them loose. This was no small task. It took me 30 minutes to loosen the tires from the ice.

Then climbing into my big truck, I placed my truck in first gear and slowly let out on the clutch. My wheels were free, but they spun on the four inches of ice they were sitting on. At this point I climbed out of my truck again and I began to pound the ice underneath my tires. I pounded repetitively, climbing in and out of my truck and crawling underneath my truck for over 30 minutes and that is when I felt pain in my low back. Two men came out from the customer's office and began pounding on the ice, too. After a few minutes one of the men went back inside. The other remained with me for additional 10 minutes, and then he returned to the building.

Once I had successfully moved the trailer, I parked it and when I pulled the fifth wheel release arm (which unhooks the trailer from the truck) I could hardly move it. I grabbed my tandem puller and lodged it against the lip of the trailer, pulling with all my strength. Finally the release arm began to move. Then the rubber tip that pressed against the lip of the trailer slipped (because it was wet from the snow and ice), lodging itself into a hole located just under the lip of the trailer, pulling the bar and release arm tight. It was stuck.

"AAAAHHHH," I groaned, pushing my face up toward the sky but shutting my eyes hard. I pulled and pulled, twisted and wrestled with it but I could not move it. I asked for a crow bar but neither the customer nor the company next door to them had one, and there was no one who offered to help me. I wrestled with the release arm for over an hour before I was able to get it loose. By this point, my shoulder and lower back began to throb with excruciating pain.

Once I dropped the empty trailer I re-hooked to my original loaded trailer, and I proceeded to pull it around the building. After all that hard work, the customer decided he wanted the load brought to a different door. However, to get around to the other side of the building I had to pull through the gate of a neighboring company who shared the parking lot.

The fence leading out around the building was only opened wide enough for a small car to pull through. I went inside to ask someone to open the gate wider. Much to my chagrin, I was informed that the gate was not electric, it was manual. The manager said, "Go for it!" This meant that I could try to move it on my own, but no one from their office was going to help me. Instead, they waited and watched the spectacle from their office windows. The snow surrounding the fence was approximately 2 feet deep or more. It was hard and compacted from the sun's melting effect during the day to the freezing ice that resulted from the colder temperatures at night. I had to physically remove the snow. I did this by using my hands and feet to clear as much snow as possible before pushing my entire body weight against the fence. I did this repetitively; each time gaining only an inch or two before starting again. I had to stop several times to allow my back to rest. By the time I had finished my entire body was in agony. The delivery that I had anticipated would take 30 minutes, had taken more than 3 hours. I was shaking and weakened by the experience.

A few hours later, I picked up my next load and began driving toward Kansas City. I was having difficulty clutching because of the pain radiating into my leg from my back. Nevertheless, I pushed onward; I did not want to get stranded someplace between Wisconsin and Kansas City. It was a grueling trip, but I managed to make it home. Four days later, still barely able to walk, I decided to go to a doctor. My doctor took me off work and designed a recovery program for my back and shoulder.

It would take me more than four months to heal from the damage I caused my body that day. Yet, the greatest healing was not of my body but of my spirit as I came to terms with the realization that *peace is,* truly, *an inward journey.* I had been saying these words for years, but now they became my mantra as I witnessed myself struggling with the things that I believed kept me from peace. I guess I had always known that I would have to reconcile the contradiction residing inside of me.

I knew the moment had come for me to deal with the artificial peace that was driving the direction of my life. Somewhere inside of me, I still believed that my happiness, my peace, was linked to my material world. As much as I hated to admit it to myself, I like so many others that I distained for doing so, believed that I could be satisfied and appeased by my physical comforts.

I knew that for me, everything came down to dollars and cents. I had not resolved this issue, that night at the casino in Reno, Nevada. I had merely touched on the issue, realizing that it was there. Even after I knew that it was "costing" me far more than it benefited me, I continued to worship the golden calf. I had remained entangled in the money snare. For all my pompous posturing, I was as much a consumer as the next person. It did not matter that I was a vegan vegetarian, or that I recycled and supported businesses that followed a more humane approach to living. My thinking was still that of a consumer—a bottom feeder! I was a glutton, a person who was disappearing into my own oblivion. I was sinking into my own abyss, far away from the experience of Peace. "Peace" remained a word in my head, a destination. It was someplace I could take a trip to, but not truly experience.

Like Jonah, I wanted Nineveh on my own terms. Jonah feared the loss of his physical safety, his reputation, and his livelihood if he entered Nineveh. I feared the same, if I were to throw all caution to the wind and enter Nineveh, where relationships are valued above all else. "Could I survive the Nineveh experience?" I wondered. I was not certain. How could I be? I was on this side of the experience.

During the four months that I was physically healing, I wrestled with my decision. Though I would say I was "finished with driving," I waffled with whether I would return to it, just temporarily until some other job hired me. "Would I go back to my whale? Would I choose another type of whale, another type of confinement to distract and take my mind off Nineveh?" I wondered.

When the day came that I needed to decide whether I would drive again, I resigned from the company. I walked away without a safety net. I had no insurance, no income, and no way of knowing what awaited me, but for the first time it did not matter. I was tired of my swallowed up, shallow existence. Like Jonah, I was ready to discover the spiritual wealth of Nineveh.

The Nineveh Experience; Opening My Heart

It was a beautiful Missouri summer's day about 6:30 a.m. and Amanda and I were preparing to sit down at the table for breakfast. As I passed one of the windows facing the backyard and pasture area, I caught a glimpse of something moving in the grass by the fence. I stopped. "What's that?" I asked inquisitively.

"What's what?" Amanda said as she hurried pass me.

"In the yard over there!" I said pointing toward the moving creature.

Amanda stopped. We both stood motionless, staring out the window. "Oh, it's a turtle" I said. "Wow it is huge. It is over a hundred feet away. That is one big turtle." I said.

"Really big!" Amanda humored me in her playful voice.

"Yeah, really big," I said, ignoring that she was

thinking I was funny or cute becoming so enamored with a turtle. "Do you realize how old it has to be to be that big?" I asked.

"Really old. You should go take a picture of it," she said smiling.

"Really?" I asked, looking at her trying to determine if she was joking with me.

"Yeah, why not?" she said. "You're right—it is big. How often will we see a turtle that old or that large again?"

I grabbed the camera from my desk and headed out into the backyard. I was so excited! "Wow, look how fast it can move," I said to myself. It had longer legs than any I had seen before. I hurried across the lawn, but as I approached, the turtle slowed down and began to pull its head inward. I stepped back. I did not want to scare it.

After a few minutes, the turtle sensed I was not a predator, and continued to walk along the fence. I flashed four or five pictures, and then lowered my camera and was content to watch the turtle. I could not explain it, but it made me happy watching it. It was beautiful. I could tell it was old, because there were smooth spots worn on its shell like none I had ever seen before. "Huh, what caused that to happen," I wondered. I walked back to the house and described my close-up view of the turtle to Amanda as she was walking out the door to leave for work.

When I re-entered the house I looked out toward the fence. Even though I could not see my new little friend, I was sure it was ok. It obviously had been around a long time and had a lot of experience at keeping itself safe. I was appreciative I had the opportunity to see it. I smiled and walked back into the house.

Later that afternoon I had to go into town. Less than a fourth of a mile from my house in the middle of the road laid a large turtle. Someone had hit it, and its broken shell and smashed body lay in a puddle of drying blood. "Ohhhh," I gasped. Immediately, I felt sick to my stomach.

"Was it my turtle?" I thought. "Was it the one that had greeted the beginning of my day and filled me with such joy?" I cringed at the thought of it. "How could people be so careless?" I raged inwardly. I could feel the heat in my chest. "How thoughtless and inhumane," I said, choking back tears. "How could someone do that to a harmless creature? That person should be ashamed," I thought wanting to punish the driver who had done this.

"Maybe it was an accident," I suggested to myself.

Yet, I quickly dismissed that possibility. "It was a turtle, not a squirrel or a rabbit darting across the road at the last minute. It was a turtle, a slow moving turtle. To hit it, a person would have to be negligent, thoughtless, or brutal," I angrily thought to myself. I was not going to give up my outrage so easily by accepting this turtle's death as an "accident".

A few hours later after finishing my errands, I drove toward home while listening to NPR (National Public Radio). As I turned onto my street, I slowed down.

"Another bombing in Iraq today has left . . ." I

ignored the speaker on the radio.

I was nearing the place where the turtle laid dead in the street. I fought my urge to look away. I wanted to know, I needed to know if it was the same turtle that had been in my yard, but I could not tell. By now, it had been hit repetitively and there was no way to distinguish it. I drove onward into my driveway. I was nauseous.

"The wounded were taken to . . ." I placed my car in park and shut off the engine; the radio silenced.

I walked into my backyard. "Was it here somewhere hiding?" I wondered. I stood in the same place looking down at the grass where I had stood several hours earlier watching the turtle. I placed my hands on the fence and looked out at my sheep grazing in the pasture. I was sad, and a deep heaviness settled in my chest.

That is when I remembered Jonah. "AHHHHHHH, will the similarities never end?" I asked frustrated. Yet, as I stood there, I recalled the ending to the Jonah story for the first time with clarity. I completely understood it; it finally made sense.

God's demonstration of mercy had violated everything that Jonah believed to be true and sacred. Jonah angrily sat waiting, hoping that God would decide to use Nineveh as a massive fireworks display, reducing all the city's inhabitants to a pile of ash. As Jonah waited, only a single plant provided him shade from the sun's sweltering heat. The author of the story said that Jonah was *grateful* for the plant. Therefore, Jonah was mindful of it, he considered it, and he appreciated it. However, by the next morning, when the plant had withered and died, Jonah was so angry over the death of the plant that he wanted to give up, to be lost forever inside of his hatred. He wanted to die.

Until now, this part of the story had always seemed confusing to me, almost as if it had been a mistake, an accident. That is because I never understood the symbolism. To Jonah, the death of the plant meant there was no "justice" in Nineveh, because it appeared as if the *undeserving* (the people of Nineveh) lived and the *deserving* (the plant) died.

Thankfully, the story does not end there. It continues with God questioning Jonah regarding his ability to have compassion, mercy, and love for a plant, yet, an inability to demonstrate the same for others. For the first time, Jonah was able to differentiate between his own face and the face of God. It is only then that Jonah realized why he had to come to Nineveh and he is unable to respond to God's questions. Jonah is left speechless, because he knows that it was never God the people of Nineveh needed to fear; it was Jonah. The Nineveh experience had been about saving Jonah from his own hostility, which was fueled by his own judgments. This is why the journey to Nineveh was more frightening to him than disobeying God, being lost at sea or being swallowed by a whale. Nineveh is the place where **all** judgments end.

Still standing in the same place where the turtle had been, I asked, "So, what does all of this mean to me?"

I did not really need to ask—I already knew. My reaction to the turtle had been no different from

Jonah's response to the plant. I was angry regarding the death of the turtle, and I lashed out inwardly with harsh thoughts of judgment toward the offending driver. However, my anger and judgments, like Jonah's, went far deeper than the death of a turtle. I could not dismiss my reaction as an isolated event; instead, it was a representation of how I lived my daily life. In that instant, I realized that Nineveh had but one purpose. I had been asked to go to Nineveh to release my judgments, and my consuming hatred against myself and others.

Now it was my turn; I stood speechless, having no more words or excuses to cover up my judgments that were fueled by my own hatred. I had come to Nineveh, like Jonah and millions of others before me, and like those who will come after me, to accept Love—to know Love. Nineveh exists for no other reason but this. Only in Nineveh can the compassionate and healing face of God be seen, which until now had been obscured from my sight by my greater desire to hate. Being in the belly of the big truck, *my whale*, I had been forced to see many realities about myself and my relationships with others. However, it was Nineveh that revealed to me that I had lived my life, like Jonah, completely void of Love.

It no longer mattered that I had performed benevolent acts of charity or kindness throughout my lifetime, because I knew what lay behind each one of those acts—a motive, a payoff, a benefit that I extracted from those things or individuals I claimed I *loved*.

Still standing in my backyard overlooking my

pasture, I had a profound thought: My journey to this point had been long. I had survived being "lost" in the sea of life, and I survived being "swallowed up" and carried in the belly of the whale. This journey had taken me 42 years, but I had made it— "I was standing on the shores of Nineveh." I was no longer asleep to my life in the bottom of the boat. Nor was I apathetic in the belly of the whale. I was wide awake, and for the first time in my life I knew what was important—every*thing* and every**one**. Life was not an acquisition. My existence had never been intended to be about gaining, taking, or hording. My *soul* and sole purpose for existing was to Love—being completely present in the moment, embracing those moments and individuals with gratitude and acceptance.

The simplicity of Jonah's plant and my turtle was that **Love** *is not* selective. Jonah was not experiencing Love when he was grateful for a plant, but hated an entire city of people and desired their destruction. Nor was I experiencing Love when I was grateful for a turtle, but hated the person who hit it, or my government for waging a war, or Paradise for their treatment, or my . . . my list was endless.

In Nineveh, I am accepting that Love is not a commodity. It is not something that I can feel in one area of my life, while hating in another area. Love is constant; it is either there or it isn't. All the lessons I had been learning on my way to Tarshish and in the belly of the whale had all been leading me, pointing me to the same conclusion: a life filled with bitterness is incapable of experiencing Love. This is not because Love does not exist, but that Love has been silenced, taken hostage by my hatred. All those senseless years I spent thinking that Peace eluded me, I realized now was only my imagination. Peace had never eluded me; I had rejected it because I refused to open my heart to Love. What I had been calling "love" was an imitation, a pretense, and I knew without the acceptance of Love, there could be no Peace.

Love is not a present tied up with red ribbon, or words spoken, or an action of any kind. These are merely expressions. Love is what remains when the event has passed, the words are forgotten, and the gift has tarnished. The only way to know that Love is present is by the Peace that is left behind when Love has been shared. Peace is the testimony to the invisible footprints of Love. I realized from that moment onward that the Peace I sought was impossible to experience without Love, and Love could not exist in my life unless, like Jonah, I opened my closed heart.

"But how? How do I open my heart? How do I find my way out of this unending war, my thirst for retribution?" I asked. The only words that came to me were the words I had read a long time ago in the New Testament, when Jesus said *"Love your enemies"* (Matt 5:44). I had read these words hundreds of times. I had heard these words spoken in numerous churches. I had even taught these words myself. Yet, I had to ask, "How? How do I show Love for or to my enemies? What does it look like to do this?" I wasn't sure I had ever really seen it or experienced it.

However, before I could ask, "How to Love my enemies?" I knew I needed to ask myself, "*Who* are my enemies?" Of course, a list of usual subjects came to mind. . . . "Terrorist, Republicans, Fundamentalists . . ." My list consisted of all those who held opposing ideas, because our philosophies, theologies, and politics did not agree. Yet, while listing them off in my head, I realized this list was too arbitrary.

First of all, I identified "my enemies" as entities and not individuals. Secondly, I identified "my enemies" as those who had issues with me and not anyone I had issues with. I recognized this as cleaver deceit. "Isn't that how it always is?" I thought. An "enemy" is always seen as someone else—someone on an *opposing* side—the *offender*. No one ever considers the "enemy" to be closer, more personal.

Yet, standing there, I knew that enemies did not only meet on foreign battle fields. I knew this was the least often place they met. No, I knew enemies met far more often on familiar battle grounds. Enemies consisted of *friends* who once professed their loyalty, only to become arch-enemies. I knew enemies consisted of those who were once married, pledging their undying, "love" only to end up hating one another vehemently. I knew enemies came from the most intimate of bonds, even attacking within the family, thus, leaving siblings and parents at odds with each other, secretly or openly detesting one another, and in some cases, not speaking to one another for years.

Who are my enemies?" I asked myself.

The answer was the same for me as for Jonah and millions of others. "Anyone who opposed me. *Any*one who dared to stand between me and the things I wanted. My enemy was anyone who was different from how I thought things *should be*. My enemy was potentially anyone." I knew this, because I knew that when others opposed me, I turned away. I withdrew emotionally and physically from them. In that moment, I recognized that this single act changes friends to foes, lovers to enemies, family to strangers.

With this understanding came a startling revelation: My wars were not philosophical, religious, or political—no war ever is. This is when I became conscious that Jonah's battle had never been with the Assyrian people, nor were mine with Iraq, the White House, my employers, my dispatchers, my family, or anyone else. My wars had always been internal private battles I had waged against myself and forced outward onto others.

I had never fully understood the importance of Loving my enemies. Nor did I understood the wisdom of Jesus' words when he instructed others to "bless" their enemies, doing "good" to them, and to "pray" for them (Matt 5:22).

"What did it mean for me to pray for my enemies?" I wondered. I knew lots of people who prayed for "sinners," asking God to bring the "wretched" persons to a religious experience. Though in my youth, I had been taught that such "prayer" was a "loving" gesture, it never felt like Love to me. No, I knew what God was asking of me went beyond prayers of duty and ritual. God was calling me to Love.

After a few moments, I realized the supremacy of this teaching. I understood that if I were to give those who were considered my "enemies" such Love, then I would never be able to treat those who I claimed to "love" with anything less than Love. This is when I understood prayer for the first time and I learned how to pray. The mystery was solved because now I understood that prayer was wanting for another *no less* than I wanted for myself. Prayer withholds nothing from another that I would want withheld from myself. Prayer was extending my hand equally to all people; no one was beyond or outside my reach of Love. I knew my prayers could no longer be filled with insensitive self righteous haughtiness or meaningless rhetoric. Rather, with my words, I would bless others regardless of who they were. Prayer was not a meaningless act; it was a physical expression of Love, an act of opening my heart.

Though these thoughts were powerful and moving for me, I secretly wondered, "Is it enough?"

My mind immediately thought of the war in Iraq, the political polarization of my country, and of crime and the hatred that plagues so many hearts. A part of me doubted that this act could be enough. Yet, I felt assurance within myself. "It is not my business to judge those events or issues that arise between others. However, it is up to me to be deeply involved in the healing of the wounds within my own life, and this is how Peace will heal our world." These words were true; I did not have control over the events happening in my world, whether in the Middle East or down the street at my neighbor's house. I was not in a position to change the mind of others—that was never my place. Nevertheless, it was my place to look deeply into my own wounds and be willing to heal.

I knew my revelations would seem naive and simplistic to those who hold an alternate interpretation of *love*. "Where can such a world exist?" I asked myself as I looked outward onto a world that seemed to prefer war instead of Peace. However, I had come to understand, like Jonah, that the only place such a world could ever exist is within the individual—within me. One day the world will have no need for war; all wars will end; but they will end only as the warring ends inside each individual heart and as each individual extends that healing outward to others. This book is part of my extending.

To get to Nineveh, I had to be willing to strip myself of my disguises and facades, not in shame, but willingly and openly. I had to let go of everything that I had ever believed to be important or significant by my world's standards and by my sense of justice. I knew that my arrival here was not the ending, but a beginning.

I realized now that Nineveh was a place where relationships reigned supreme. Nothing else mattered here but my connection to others and theirs to me. This is the beauty of the Nineveh story: In Nineveh I will find the murderer, the profane, the hideous and more and I will learn, as Jonah did, to Love them—Love them all. I will come face to face with those who have hated me and wished me dead, and I will embrace them. Nineveh is the place that bitter enemies come to find each other and accept one another.

In short, Nineveh is a Love story: It is the place I learn that God's skin can not be pierced as the Earth's. I can not stab a flag into God and claim God as my own. No, this story is richer and more meaningful than my individual biases. This is a story about God not identified by a religious name or as an emblem of a particular people. It is a story where God brings others together; joining them. Nineveh is a place where all prejudice and hatred ceases to exit. Nineveh is the place where mercy lives forever and a day. Nineveh is a place where the truth is heard, regardless of the words that are spoken by an angered and bitter prophet. Nineveh is the place where Love resides. Nineveh is the place where God expresses unwavering, undying, eternal love for every person and beast. Nineveh is the home of every individual heart, and that is why we must all journey there. Nineveh is where I learn that opening my heart is opening myself to life. Nineveh is the place I learn to **Love my enemies** and recognize that they were only representations of **my *need* to Love**.

There is no mention that the character of Jonah ever left Nineveh. It is my opinion that he never did. I believe he stayed there, living out the remainder of his life learning to Love life instead of death. This is what I decided to do, too. For the first time during this entire journey, I am no longer content to stand on the other side of the door, squinting to look through the key hole. No, instead today I turn the knob and open the door, swinging it open wide. I feel the radiant Love that was always there and I bask in its light. . . . Before Nineveh, I was blinded to my prejudices and biases hiding behind the cloak of my religious piety or my "do-gooder" image. Today, that has all changed. I stand on the shores of Nineveh and I realize there is so much to Love. . . .

The Biblical city of Nineveh is no longer known or called by the name of Nineveh. Today, it is known by the name of Mosul. It is the second largest city located in modern day Iraq. I find this point particularly poignant. Not only does the Jonah experience exist on an individual level, it exists collectively. This makes sense when one considers, that the collective masses of the world are but millions upon millions of individuals. Of course, it stands to reason that world politics can only reflect what is representative in the lives of the individuals who make up those societies. Thus, the Jonah story has never changed; it continues to this day. God is still asking individuals to open their hearts to Love. God is gently calling . . . "Are you ready Jonah? Are *you*? Are you *Jonah*?"

I know now that there are many Jonahs' and joyces' in the world and not all of us reside in the "belly of a whale" or the "belly of a big truck." I write this story for all of us, that we may find our way to Nineveh.

About the Photographer

Charles Hackworth is a gifted and innovative artist. He currently, resides in Arizona. You can learn more about him and view his artwork on his website at www.ofthislife.com or you can email him at PhotographerAZ@aol.com

About the Author

joyce cascio's life's work is dedicated to inspiring and challenging the human heart. She travels the country answering requests for speaking engagements and for facilitating workshops that promote Peace, Tolerance, and the Nineveh Experience. She lives on a small farm in Missouri with her family, and 4 sheep, 6 ducks, 2 cats, a dog, and a raccoon.

If you would like to contact joyce cascio you may email her at joyce@jonahandme.com Or visit her website at www.jonahandme.com You may also write to her at

joyce cascio
P O Box 1298
Kearney, MO 64060